"*Faithful Theology* seeks to help basis. Graham Cole sets forth a good theology—a method that, Bible and, second, shows how theologians throughout history have best used the Bible to edify the church. I am impressed with the conciseness of *Faithful Theology*. Cole has done an excellent job summarizing the basics in this short volume."

> **John M. Frame,** Professor of Systematic Theology and Philosophy Emeritus, Reformed Theological Seminary, Orlando; author, *Systematic Theology* and *A History of Western Philosophy and Theology*

"Graham Cole has enviable gifts of clarity and wisdom, combined with an ability to identify significant themes in theology. *Faithful Theology* is as fresh, bright, and crisp as a sun-drenched spring morning. It is as helpful for connecting the dots in Christian discipleship in the church as it is for pastoral formation in the seminary context. It is profound in its simplicity."

> **C. Ben Mitchell,** Graves Professor of Moral Philosophy, Union University

"We are all theologians, and we all practice theology, good or bad. Ministers and lay people need to learn how to do theology, to think theologically, to increase our theological awareness and theological ability, and to think God's thoughts after him. We need to do this not only to understand our past but also to work through new issues of today and tomorrow. Graham Cole writes with his usual clarity and has provided a resource that is short, deep, vivid, and thoughtful! He shows us a method of doing faithful theology. This method requires honoring and using the Bible and the insights of the past, as well as clarity of thought, an understanding of sin and frustration, humility, patience, faith, prayer, and worship. We see these features reflected in this book."

> **Peter Adam,** Vicar Emeritus, St Jude's Church, Carlton; Former Principal, Ridley College, Melbourne

"This helpful primer provides the common sense, plain speech, biblical perspective, and evangelical commitment we've come to expect from Graham Cole."

Daniel J. Treier, Gunther H. Knoedler Professor of Theology, Wheaton College; author, *Introducing Evangelical Theology*

"Drawing from his years of teaching, Graham A. Cole guides the reader like a pastoral sage. *Faithful Theology* offers much insightful discussion about how to wed the demand for contextual affirmation and a commitment to scriptural authority. Cole is to be thanked for illustrating how we need to do theology as pilgrims heading home."

Andrew J. Schmutzer, Professor of Bible, Moody Bible Institute; author, *Between Pain and Grace: A Biblical Theology of Suffering*

Faithful Theology

SHORT STUDIES IN SYSTEMATIC THEOLOGY

Edited by Graham A. Cole and Oren R. Martin

Faithful Theology

An Introduction

Graham A. Cole

WHEATON, ILLINOIS

Faithful Theology: An Introduction

Copyright © 2020 by Graham A. Cole

Published by Crossway
      1300 Crescent Street
      Wheaton, Illinois 60187

Cover design: Jordan Singer

Cover image: From the New York Public Library, catalog ID (B-number): b14500417

First printing 2020

Printed in the United States of America

Trade paperback ISBN: 978-1-4335-5911-2
ePub ISBN: 978-1-4335-5914-3
PDF ISBN: 978-1-4335-5912-9
Mobipocket ISBN: 978-1-4335-5913-6

Library of Congress Cataloging-in-Publication Data

Names: Cole, Graham A. (Graham Arthur), 1949– author.
Title: Faithful theology: an introduction / Graham A. Cole.
Description: Wheaton: Crossway, 2020. | Series: Short studies in systematic theology | Includes
    bibliographical references and index.
Identifiers: LCCN 2019020276 (print) | ISBN 9781433559112 (tp)
Subjects: LCSH: Bible—Hermeneutics. | Theology.
Classification: LCC BS476 .C57 2020 (print) | LCC BS476 (ebook) | DDC 230—dc23
LC record available at https://lccn.loc.gov/2019020276
LC ebook record available at https://lccn.loc.gov/2019981073

Crossway is a publishing ministry of Good News Publishers.

VP			30	29	28	27	26	25	24	23	22	21	20
15	14	13	12	11	10	9	8	7	6	5	4	3	2	1

To the many, many students
I have taught this method to
on three continents

Contents

Series Preface

The ancient Greek thinker Heraclitus reputedly said that the thinker has to listen to the essence of things. A series of theological studies dealing with the traditional topics that make up systematic theology needs to do just that. Accordingly, in these studies, theologians address the essence of a doctrine. This series thus aims to present short studies in theology that are attuned to both the Christian tradition and contemporary theology in order to equip the church to faithfully understand, love, teach, and apply what God has revealed in Scripture about a variety of topics. What may be lost in comprehensiveness can be gained through what Calvin, in the dedicatory epistle of his commentary on Romans, called "lucid brevity."

Of course, a thorough study of any doctrine will be longer rather than shorter, as there are two millennia of confession, discussion, and debate with which to interact. As a result, a short study needs to be more selective, but deftly so. Thankfully, the contributors to this series have the ability to be brief yet accurate. The key aim is that the simpler is not to morph into the simplistic. The test is whether the topic of a short study, when further studied in depth, requires some unlearning to take place. The simple can be amplified. The simplistic needs to be corrected. As editors, we believe that the volumes in this series pass that test.

While the specific focus will vary, each volume will (1) introduce the doctrine, (2) set it in context, (3) develop it from Scripture, (4) draw the various threads together, and (5) bring it to bear on the Christian life. It is our prayer, then, that this series will assist the church to delight in her triune God by thinking his thoughts—which he has graciously revealed in his written word, which testifies to his living Word, Jesus Christ—after him in the powerful working of his Spirit.

Graham A. Cole and Oren R. Martin

Introduction

The case can be made that every Christian is a theologian because every Christian has a theology, whether well thought out or not.[1] After all, the word "theology" clearly has to do with God (*theos*, Greek for "God"), and since the third century at least, theology has been understood to refer to "talking about God" (*theos*, "God"; *logos*, "word").[2] When that talk is organized, we have a body of teaching, or doctrine. Some become highly trained in talking about God and in thinking about him in a systematic way. Others, because of calling or life circumstance, never have much chance to develop that level of expertise. Whether trained or not, Christians talk and think about God. In that light, there is a sense in which every Christian is a theologian. The question is, How are we to get better at talking and thinking about God? That question brings us to the matter of method. But what is a method? Theologian Robert W. Jenson explains it well: "A method, of course, is a self-conscious

---

1. For an example of an attempt to make that case, see Stanley J. Grenz and Roger E. Olson, *Who Needs Theology? An Invitation to the Study of God* (Downers Grove, IL: InterVarsity Press, 1996). Their first chapter is titled "Everyone Is a Theologian." In my view, they paint with too broad a brush. They contend, "Anyone who reflects on life's ultimate questions—including questions about God and our relationship to God—is a theologian" (13). For them, filmmaker and actor Woody Allen qualifies as one (14). Given their definitions, it is hard to see the difference between a theologian and a philosopher.

2. See Alister E. McGrath, *Theology: The Basics*, 3rd ed. (Chichester, UK: Wiley-Blackwell, 2012), xii.

way of going about doing something."[3] This book is about the method to use in doing faithful theology: faithful to God, faithful to God's word.

When I was a lad, my uncle Gordon showed me how to catch more fish with a rod and reel. Before he tied the hook on the line, he attached a much smaller hook that was free. The big hook was put through the bait or hidden in it. Next, the little hook was placed through the tail of the shrimp or other bait. He called it the keeper hook. Over the years, I have caught some really big fish on that little hook alone. My uncle gave me a way of being better at fishing. He gave me a technique, a better fishing method. He taught me how to improve my fishing success. What he did reminds me of an old piece of wisdom: It is better to teach someone how to fish than simply to give that person a fish. The difference is satisfying the hunger of the day versus having a way to satisfy hunger over a lifetime. Method matters, and not only for practical things like fishing, but also for finding out the truth of things, especially the things of God.[4]

When it comes to the truth of the things of God, Scripture plays the pivotal role as God's self-revelation. (I shall argue this at length in chapter 1.) Indeed, faithful theology is a human project that arises from wise reflection on the self-revelation of God.[5] Because it is our reflection on God's revelation, it is always open to be reformed and corrected by that revelation.

---

3. Robert W. Jenson, *A Theology in Outline: Can These Bones Live?* (Oxford, UK: Oxford University Press, 2016), 111.

4. The philosopher René Descartes (1596–1650) knew that method matters and that the mind needs direction. He had twenty-one rules. Here is his fourth: "We need a method if we are to investigate the truth of things." Descartes, "Rules for the Direction of the Mind," Wikisource (website), https://en.wikisource.org/wiki/Rules_for_the_Direction_of_the_Mind, accessed March 16, 2017.

5. I take a different view than do Grenz and Olson on the question of the object of theologizing. They argue in *Who Needs Theology?*, 49, that "Christian theology is reflecting on and articulating the God-centered life and beliefs that Christians share as followers of Jesus Christ, and it is done in order that God may be glorified in all Christians are to do." This is far too anthropocentric in my view. The primary object of theological reflection is God, not our beliefs per se.

This is the truth of the Reformers' slogan *semper reformanda* (always reforming). However, it is one thing to have an evangelical's high view of Scripture. It is quite another to know how to derive teaching (doctrine or theology) from Scripture.[6]

We need guidance just as I needed guidance from Uncle Gordon. The need to do so is easily illustrated. I was taught as a new Christian that when Jesus slept in the boat during the storm on the Sea of Galilee, his human side was showing itself. But when he rose up and commanded the storm to cease, his divine side was expressing itself. It was as though Jesus's two natures oscillated, first the human and then the divine, taking turns. Later, when I was taught some theology and how to evaluate theological proposals, I saw that this was very much like the ancient heresy of Nestorianism. On this view, Jesus was both a human person and a divine person. The Father had, in effect, two sons in one physical body.[7] However, if Scripture is compared with Scripture, and if the witness of the early church fathers is taken into account, then Jesus is clearly one person and not two. As one person, he had both a truly human nature and a truly divine one at all times.

This brief work especially explores how such a move from Scripture to doctrine is made. But why does doctrine matter? The importance of doctrine lies in that it answers three normative questions vital to us all: (1) What ought we to believe (*orthodoxy*, right opinion)? This is the truth question. (2) What ought we to value (*orthokardia*, right-heartedness)? This is the

---

6. I am using "doctrine," "teaching," and "theology" as synonyms.

7. Nestorianism is a wrong view (heresy) of Jesus named after Nestorius (386–451), bishop of Constantinople. Nestorius allegedly taught that the incarnate Christ was two persons: one human and one divine. Whether he actually held the view associated with his name is still debated. See H. D. McDonald, "Nestorius (fl. 428–c. 451)," in *New Dictionary of Theology Historical and Systematic*, 2nd ed., ed. Martin Davie, Tim Grass, Stephen R. Holmes, John McDowell, and T. A. Noble (Downers Grove, IL: InterVarsity Press, 2016), 609–10. Chap. 2 of the book before you aims to show the value of knowing facts like these.

spirituality question. (3) How ought we to live (*orthopraxy*, right practice of life)? This is the existential or practical question. Put another way, the head (orthodoxy), the heart (orthokardia), and the hands (orthopraxy) all count as concerns of theology. For example, what ought we to believe about the identity of Jesus? Does our answer matter? How are we to live in the light of Jesus's identity? If you believed, as many do, that Jesus was merely human, then worshiping him would be idolatry. But if Jesus is a member of the Holy Trinity, then worship is entirely fitting.[8]

To answer thoroughly the above questions, five key elements are involved.[9] In this work, a chapter is devoted to each. Chapter 1 explores the foundation of theology in the self-witness of God in Scripture. This element is "The Word of Revelation." However, God has been providentially at work in the history of theological debate and discussion. As German theologian Gerhard Ebeling says, Scripture construed as the word of God has been central to that conversation. He argues that the history of the church is the history of the exposition of the Bible in the church.[10] Knowledge of that conversation is another important element in doing theology, as chapter 2, "The Witness of Christian Thought and Practice," seeks to show. The third chapter recognizes that we do theology in a context. We live outside of Eden in the new normal, or abnormal. There is brokenness about us and in us. This element is

---

8. The doctrine of the Trinity will be the key case in point to which I shall return at numerous places throughout this book. I completed a first draft of this work before I read Grenz and Olson, *Who Needs Theology?* In that work they also make frequent reference to the doctrine of the Trinity to support many of their points.

9. In one sense every believer is a theologian with thoughts about God and God's relation to the world. Some believers have an unreflective theology. Some have a reflective theology. Hopefully, a college course necessitates reflection. Others have a mission-informed theology and want to be able to teach the church as trained pastors and theologians.

10. Gerhard Ebeling, *The Word of God and Tradition: Historical Studies Interpreting the Divisions of Christianity*, trans. S. H. Hooke (Philadelphia: Fortress, 1968), 11.

"The World of Human Brokenness." Bringing these elements together requires wisdom from God. Chapter 4 investigates the role of wisdom in doing theology. This element is "The Work of Wisdom."[11] Finally, chapter 5 tackles the question of how the various elements are to be put together. It summarizes the discussion and affirms the doxological dimension in doing theology. This element can be summed up as "The Way of Worship." That is to say, our doing theology ought to be an offering to God.

Is it worth the effort? Does method matter? Gregory Boyd and Paul Eddy rightly state: "A central debate among evangelical theologians concerns the question of theological method. In other words, how should we 'do' theology?"[12] To get our idea of God right we need the right method of doing theology. As we have seen, "theology" is a term made up of two others: *theos* (for "God") and *logos* (for "word" or "discourse").

Doing theology aright matters. But that does not mean that this work is written to the academic guild. I write as a church scholar. Such a work may be of use to the guild, but in the first instance it is addressed to pastors, theological students, college students, and interested layfolk. I have written simply but, I hope, not simplistically. What's the difference? A simple work

---

11. Some of these elements appear in Albert Outler's famous formulation of the Wesleyan Quadrilateral. His formulation gave the impression that, for John Wesley, Scripture stood on an equal footing with tradition, reason, and experience. However, as Outler later made clear, this was an unfortunate way of characterizing Wesley's theology: "The term 'quadrilateral' does not occur in the Wesley corpus—and more than once I have regretted having coined it for contemporary use since it has been so widely misconstrued." Quoted in Jonathan Andersen, "The Myth of the 'Wesleyan Quadrilateral,'" http://www.jonathanandersen.com/the-myth-of-the-wesleyan-quadrilateral/, accessed November 6, 2017. For Wesley, Scripture was the supreme authority, and the other three were subordinate to the Bible. The original formulation is found in Albert Outler, "The Wesleyan Quadrilateral—in John Wesley," in *The Wesleyan Theological Heritage: Essays of Albert C. Outler*, ed. Thomas C. Oden and Leicester R. Longden (Grand Rapids, MI: Zondervan, 1991), 26.

12. Gregory A. Boyd and Paul R. Eddy, *Across the Spectrum: Understanding Issues in Evangelical Theology*, 2nd ed. (Grand Rapids, MI: Baker Academic, 2009), 293.

is more accessible for a wider readership than a highly technical one would be. Yet the technically proficient may still be able to flesh out its ideas and run with them. A simplistic work keeps breaking down in logic and usefulness the more one knows about the field and, above all, the text of Scripture.

1

The Word of Revelation

Last century A. W. Tozer wrote:

> What comes into our minds when we think about God
> is the most important thing about us. . . . The history of
> mankind will probably show that no people has ever risen
> above its religion, and man's spiritual history will positively
> demonstrate that no religion has ever been greater than its
> idea of God. . . . Always the most revealing thing about the
> Church is her idea of God, just as her most significant mes-
> sage is what she says about Him or leaves unsaid, for her si-
> lence is often more eloquent than her speech. She can never
> escape the self-disclosure of her witness concerning God.[1]

Tozer's bold claims beg an important question: Where ought
the church get its ideas of God?

In my first semester of theological study I happened to meet
someone I knew from my undergraduate days in the campus Christian group. We shared our new experiences of being at different,

---

1. A. W. Tozer, *The Knowledge of the Holy* (San Francisco: HarperSanFrancisco,
1961), 1. Tozer is an example of a self-taught theologian (an autodidact), of which there
are very few. The famous nineteenth-century preacher Charles Spurgeon was another.

very different, theological colleges. He was in his first year too. I remarked how my doctrine class was all about grounding our theological claims in Scripture. He too had studied doctrine that semester, and the Bible had not been opened once. Instead, the class worked its way through a text by the eminent liberal theologian Paul Tillich, who was all the rage in that college.

I could not help but think that my former schoolmate was being given stones to eat and not bread. How different was my evangelical theology teacher Broughton Knox. He was clear that our ideas of God are to be found in the self-revelation of God and that the self-revelation of God is to be found in Scripture. Any doctrine that had no biblical warrant he described as "a textless doctrine" and not worthy to be called doctrine.[2] Doing theology is an evidence-based practice, and Scripture provides the crucial evidence.[3]

The text of Scripture is vital to doing theology in an evangelical way. Why? Because God has spoken and unveiled his mind, his will, and his ways (Heb. 1:1–2). Scripture is the Spirit-inspired, inerrant, and infallible crystallization of the divine discourse. Paul writes to his younger associate Timothy in these terms (2 Tim. 3:14–17):

> But as for you, continue in what you have learned and have firmly believed, knowing from whom you learned it and how from childhood you have been acquainted with the sacred writings, which are able to make you wise for salvation through faith in Christ Jesus. All Scripture is breathed

---

2. My institution is affiliated with the Evangelical Free Church of America (EFCA). Historically for this denomination, "The test for all doctrine and deportment was the Scriptures. 'Where stands it written?' . . . was the battle cry in all controversies." See Arnold Theodore Olson, *Stumbling Towards Maturity* (Minneapolis: Free Church Press, 1981), 159.

3. Evidence is that which counts toward deciding the truth or falsity of a claim. See Richard Feldman, "Evidence," in *The Cambridge Dictionary of Philosophy*, 2nd ed., ed. Robert Audi (Cambridge, UK: Cambridge University Press, 1999), 293.

out [*theopneustos*, "God-breathed"] by God and profitable for teaching, for reproof, for correction, and for training in righteousness, that the man of God may be complete, equipped for every good work.

Scripture has its origins in God like no other book or collection of books (e.g., the canon of Shakespeare's works). It is *theopneustos* (God-breathed), as 2 Timothy 3:16 argues. Apparently, Paul had to coin this new word in Greek to capture the divine role in producing Scripture. G. C. Berkouwer is correct in affirming that "Paul's word . . . points to a unique origin and to a unique relation of Holy Scripture to God."[4] *Theopneustos* refers to an objective reality, not a subjective one. In many ways, the term "inspired" is not strong enough and is indeed misleading.[5] I have a friend who is an expert in all things Shakespearean. She would say that the canon of Shakespeare's works is inspired in its ability to move the human spirit. That is a subjective understanding of the term. In contrast, *theopneustos* puts Scripture in a category apart.

"Inerrant" means that Scripture teaches no errors. Inerrancy has to do with Scripture's content.[6] "Infallible" means that Scripture won't lead astray. Infallibility has to do with God's purpose in giving Scripture to his people. Put in positive terms, Scripture is trustworthy and truth-telling. Someone might object that I have anthropomorphized Scripture as though it were a person. If so, I have an apostolic precedent in Paul, who wrote to the Galatians in these terms: "And the Scripture, foreseeing that God would justify the Gentiles by faith, preached the gospel beforehand to Abraham, saying, 'In you shall all the

---

4. G. C. Berkouwer, *Studies in Dogmatics: Holy Scripture*, trans. and ed. Jack B. Rogers (Grand Rapids, MI: Eerdmans, 1975), 140.

5. Both the ESV and NIV translate *theopneustos* as "God-breathed" and are to be preferred to the NRSV on this point.

6. Inerrancy could be explored by a monograph in its own right. For our purposes, suffice it to say that the reference point is the Chicago Statement on Biblical Inerrancy, http://www.bible-researcher.com/chicago1.html, accessed February 22, 2017.

nations be blessed'" (3:8). Likewise, these words of Paul to the Roman Christians in Romans 9:17 are particularly noteworthy: "For Scripture says to Pharaoh . . ." Paul then quotes Exodus 9:16, where God is the speaker. A text like Romans 9:17 informs the claim that what Scripture says, God says.[7]

The human dimension of Scripture must also be taken into account, as 2 Peter 1:21 makes plain: "For no prophecy was ever produced by the will of man, but men spoke from God as they were carried along by the Holy Spirit." It is obvious upon reading the New Testament that human authors were at work: the idiom of Paul is very different from that of John, for example. A mysterious double agency has produced Scripture. There is a human story to be told of Paul and John, but there is also the divine story of the Holy Spirit's primary authorship. That primary authorship can especially be seen in Hebrews 10:15–17 and its use of Jeremiah 31:33–34:

> And the Holy Spirit also bears witness to us; for after saying,
>
> > "This is the covenant that I will make with them
> >   after those days, declares the Lord:
> > I will put my laws on their hearts,
> >   and write them on their minds,"
>
> then he adds,
>
> > "I will remember their sins and their lawless deeds
> >   no more."[8]

---

7. B. B. Warfield appeals to both Gal. 3:8 and Rom. 9:17, among other texts, in his chapter titled "'It Says:' 'Scripture Says:' 'God Says,'" in his *The Inspiration and Authority of the Bible*, ed. Samuel G. Craig (Philadelphia: Presbyterian and Reformed, 1970), 299–348.

8. It is worth noting that "then he adds" is not in the Greek text. The force of the language is instructive. Not only, according to the writer to the Hebrews, did the Holy Spirit speak these words; they have continuing impact and relevance to a first-century readership (and to us).

Theologian Kevin Vanhoozer captures the duality of Scripture in a particularly clear and helpful way when he writes:

> The Bible is both like and unlike every other text. It is like every other book because it has human authors who say something about something in some way. It is *unlike* every other book because (1) it has God for its ultimate author; (2) it has God (Jesus Christ) as its ultimate content; (3) it has God (the Holy Spirit) for its ultimate interpreter; and (4) it has the church for its ultimate interpretive community.[9]

This is finely said and notable for the way Vanhoozer articulates the duality within a Trinitarian frame of reference.

Evangelical Theology and Liberal Theology: A Key Difference

One of the issues over which liberal theology and evangelical theology part company is the inerrancy of Scripture. Stephen Sykes states the liberal position with admirable clarity: "Liberalism in theology is that mood or cast of mind which is prepared to accept that some discovery of reason may count *against* the authority of a traditional affirmation in the body of Christian theology."[10] He goes on to write of "autonomously functioning reason."[11] To illustrate his point, he selects the traditional affirmation of the doctrine of Scripture. He writes: "For most Protestant Christians the most momentous step of theological liberalism is taken when they deny the traditionally accepted belief in the inerrancy of Scripture."[12] F. H. Cleobury argues similarly:

---

9. Kevin J. Vanhoozer, "From Bible to Theology," in *Theology, Church, and Ministry: A Handbook for Theological Education*, ed. David S. Dockery (Nashville: B&H Academic, 2017), 239; original emphasis.

10. Stephen Sykes, *Christian Theology Today* (London and Oxford: Mowbray, 1983), 12; original emphasis.

11. Sykes, *Christian Theology Today*, 12.

12. Sykes, *Christian Theology Today*, 12.

Another way of answering the question, "What is liberal-ism?" is to consider the question, "Why do we believe the Christian religion to be the highest revelation from God to man?" If a person replies, "I believe it because it is taught by an infallible authority," whether he means the Pope, the Church or the Bible, *he is not a liberal*.[13]

Cleobury is quite explicit about evangelicals: "And some of my conservative evangelical friends seem to think that the neces-sary and sufficient reason for believing anything in the field of religion is that it can be 'Proved from Scripture'."[14] Clearly, Cleobury would take major issue with this particular book.

A robust evangelical doctrine of Scripture construes Scrip-ture in a threefold way: (1) Scripture is the definitive source for our knowledge of God: his character, will, and ways. (2) Scrip-ture is the verbally inspired, definitive witness to the words and acts of God in history. (3) Scripture is not only a source and a witness but also the norm by which theological proposals are to be tested. In terms of authority, Scripture is the *norma normans* (norming norm).

Bibliology and Christology

There is the closest of connections between our Bibliology (doc-trine of the Book) and our Christology (doctrine of the person and work of Christ) at this point. Jesus lived by every word that proceeded out of the mouth of God as his encounter with the devil in the wilderness shows in Matthew 4:1–11 (about which I'll say more later, p. 31). Jesus also encountered human opposition to his mission from Pharisees and Sadducees. His debate on one occasion with some Sadducees is instructive. Jesus was presented

---

13. F. H. Cleobury, *Liberal Christian Orthodoxy* (London: James Clarke, 1963), 14; my emphasis.
14. Cleobury, *Liberal Christian Orthodoxy*, 15.

with a conundrum: If a woman dies having been married many times, whose wife will she be in the resurrection? The Sadducees didn't actually believe in the resurrection, so their aim was to show up Jesus as foolish. Jesus's response is striking (Matt. 22:29–32):

> But Jesus answered them, "You are wrong, because you know neither the Scriptures nor the power of God. For in the resurrection they neither marry nor are given in marriage, but are like angels in heaven. And as for the resurrection of the dead, have you not read what was said to you by God: 'I am the God of Abraham, and the God of Isaac, and the God of Jacob'? He is not God of the dead, but of the living."

For a start, notice that Jesus believed that you can err theologically ("You are wrong"), which is an unpopular idea in a relativistic age like ours. The Sadducees' formal error was not believing the Scriptures. These Jews prized the books of Moses, so Jesus quoted from Exodus 3:6 as his case in point.[15] Their material error was not reckoning with the content and implications of the very part of the Old Testament that they believed. Exodus 3:6 implies that Abraham, Isaac, and Jacob were in some sense alive in the presence of God. God is, not was, the God of all three. No wonder the crowds were amazed at Jesus's teaching (Matt. 22:33).

Moreover, Jesus did not simply make a statement about their error; he asked a penetrating question: "Have you not read . . . ?" It would be strange indeed if the follower of Christ had a lesser view of Scripture than the Christ he or she claimed to follow.[16] Scripture needs to be read accordingly, that is to say,

---

15. Logically speaking, Jesus employed a non-fallacious form of the ad hominem argument. He used the very Scripture the Sadducees regarded as authoritative to reveal that the text had consequences that undermined their position.

16. This is not a work of apology (defense). Instead, it is a work of clarification. It seeks to clarify theological method. Apologetics is a different discipline with different methods. Apologetics is a work of justification. It seeks to show the justification for Christianity's truth claims, including truth claims about the Bible (its authority,

with high confidence: read for sense, read for sustenance, and read for its doctrine. To use the classic evangelical metaphor, Scripture is the touchstone of faith. Scripture provides quality assurance when it comes to testing whether our theological proposals are real gold or fool's gold. Bishop J. C. Ryle (1816–1900) serves as an example. He wrote:

> Let me first of all ask every one who reads this paper, to arm himself with a thorough knowledge of the written Word of God. Unless we do this we are at the mercy of any false teacher. We shall not see through the mistakes of an erring Peter. We shall not be able to imitate the faithfulness of a courageous Paul. An ignorant laity will always be the bane of a Church. A Bible-reading laity may save a Church from ruin. Let us read the Bible regularly, daily, and with fervent prayer, and become familiar with its contents. Let us receive nothing, believe nothing, follow nothing, which is not in the Bible, nor can be proved by the Bible. Let our rule of faith, *our touchstone of all teaching*, be the written Word of God.[17]

In this quote, Ryle exemplifies the classical evangelical tradition in its high view of Scripture as he warns churches of the dangers of abandoning belief in the Bible's authority.

The Matter of Interpretation (Hermeneutics)

It is one thing, though, to have a high view of the Bible's verbal inspiration and authority. It is another to interpret Scripture aright. Is the Bible to be read like no other book or like every

inspiration, inerrancy, canonicity, etc.). For a work of apology, see D. A. Carson, ed., *The Enduring Authority of the Christian Scriptures* (Grand Rapids, MI: Eerdmans, 2016).

17. J. C. Ryle, "The Fallibility of Ministers," chap. 6 in *Warnings to the Churches* (London: Banner of Truth, 1967), http://www.nrcrws.org/warnings-to-churches.htm, accessed May 4, 2019; my emphasis. A "touchstone" was an assaying tool for testing whether gold or silver is genuine. A fine-grained piece of quartz or jasper will leave a particular color streak when the ore is marked with it.

other book? R. C. Sproul is one theologian who recognized how we need to read Scripture. He wrote:

> Over time I have not only learned about God but I learned the proper rules for reading his Word so that I could understand correctly who this God is, what he demands, and what he has done for sinners. Learning how to read the Scripture, I dare say, was as important as reading the Bible itself. My reading of sacred Scripture from cover to cover and growth in understanding of how to read the Bible correctly—is what defined my theology and my entire career of teaching and preaching the Word of God.[18]

The question is, How are we to read Scripture in a way that retrieves its true sense? Regarding this, I believe that the hermeneutic of the Reformers of the sixteenth century is still instructive for us: Scripture interprets Scripture, Scripture is not to be interpreted against Scripture, and plain Scripture is to interpret obscure Scripture.[19]

Scripture interpreting Scripture is predicated on the idea that the primary author of Scripture is the Holy Spirit working concursively with human authors. There is thus a unity to divine self-revelation. The book of Hebrews affirms this double agency as can be seen where the writer uses Psalm 95 to encourage the Jewish Christian readers to stay true to Christ and not to drift away because of hostile societal pressure. In Hebrews 3:7 we read, "Therefore, as the Holy Spirit says, 'Today, if you hear his voice.'" The writer proceeds to quote Psalm 95 at length. Hebrews 3:7–11, therefore, is clearly asserting that Psalm 95 is the Spirit's speech. In the next chapter the human

---

18. R. C. Sproul, *Knowing Scripture*, 3rd ed. (Downers Grove, IL: InterVarsity Press, 2016), 11. Sproul's book is an excellent contemporary introduction to hermeneutics that is scholarly but accessible in that the scholarship is not obtrusive.

19. Sproul, *Knowing Scripture*, 51–53. Sproul also highly values the Reformers' hermeneutic.

dimension comes to the fore. In Hebrews 4:7, we learn that this word was spoken through David:

> Again he appoints a certain day, "Today," saying through David so long afterward, in the words already quoted,
>
>> "Today, if you hear his voice,
>> do not harden your hearts."

Dual authorship is also in view in 2 Peter 1:21, which asserts with reference to Scripture that men spoke for God as they were moved by the Holy Spirit.

That Scripture is not to be interpreted against Scripture also assumes that the Holy Spirit, as the primary author of Scripture, knows what he is doing and that there is a consistency in truth telling in Scripture. After all, Scripture describes the Holy Spirit as the Spirit of truth. This claim does not mean that everything is straightforward in Scripture and easy to interpret. There are difficulties and tensions. On the relation of faith and works, does James 2 contradict Ephesians 2? I think not, because these texts are addressing different pastoral needs. But analysis and careful exegesis are needed to show this. The all-too-facile move is to pit biblical author against biblical author. Although in my view Barth did not have a biblically robust doctrine of Scripture, he was right in advising students on the occasion of his farewell before his expulsion from Germany in 1935: "And now the end has come. So listen to my piece of advice: exegesis, exegesis, and yet more exegesis! Keep to the Word, to the Scripture that has been given to us."[20]

---

20. Quoted in Gordon Fee, *New Testament Exegesis: A Handbook for Students and Pastors*, 3rd ed. (Louisville: Westminster, 2002), v. I heard this wise remark years ago: "Have many teachers but only one Master." The evangelical ought to be open to wisdom from any source, yet under the lordship of Christ.

The last Reformation interpretive, or hermeneutical, principle to note is that of allowing the plain Scripture to interpret the obscure Scripture. There are things difficult to understand in Scripture, as Peter claims with Paul's writings in view (2 Pet. 3:15–16):

> And count the patience of our Lord as salvation, just as our beloved brother Paul also wrote to you according to the wisdom given him, as he does in all his letters when he speaks in them of these matters. There are some things in them that are hard to understand, which the ignorant and unstable twist to their own destruction, as they do the other Scriptures.

This is such an interesting statement. Peter puts Paul's letters in the category of Scripture. Moreover, he acknowledges that there is a level of interpretative difficulty in Paul's letters and that they can be misused. Whatever is meant by the perspicuity, or clarity, of Scripture needs to take statements like this one into account.[21] For example, what does being baptized on behalf of the dead mean in 1 Corinthians 15:29? The Corinthian readers obviously would have known, but do we? It appears to have been a practice at Corinth, and Paul makes an appeal to it to bolster belief in the bodily resurrection of believers. He does not refer to the practice in any of his other letters that we have. It would be methodologically perilous to build a doctrine on one such obscure statement, though some do.[22]

---

21. For a recent examination of the clarity issue, see Mark D. Thompson, "The Generous Gift of a Gracious Father: Toward a Theological Account of the Clarity of Scripture," in Carson, *Enduring Authority*, 615–43. Also, see Graham Cole, "Sola Scriptura: Some Historical and Contemporary Perspectives," 29: "The majority Protestant view understood the analogy of faith as the analogy of the whole Scripture (*analogia totius Scripturae*)." https://biblicalstudies.org.uk/pdf/churchman/104-01_020.pdf, accessed March 16, 2017.

22. For the Mormon use of 1 Cor. 15:29 to justify proxy baptism, see "1 Corinthians 15–16," The Church of Jesus Christ of Latter-Day Saints (website), https://www.lds.org/manual/new-testament-student-manual/1-corinthians/chapter-40-1-corinthians-15-16?lang=eng, accessed March 23, 2017.

The classic analogy-of-faith hermeneutic, however, needs nuancing. This nuancing recognizes the role of genre in a wise reading strategy. Scripture is to be interpreted genre by genre by genre. R. C. Sproul offers great wisdom on this matter. One of the illustrations he uses concerns Adam as portrayed in Genesis. He writes: "The opening chapters of Genesis provide real difficulty to the person who wants to pinpoint the precise literary genre used. Part of the text has the earmarks of historical literature, yet part of it exhibits the kind of imagery found in symbolic literature."[23] He concludes, "Only after we determine what kind of literature it is can we discern what it is communicating to us as history."[24]

Bible-believing readers of Scripture may disagree at the level of genre identification without disagreeing as to the authority of Scripture as God's word written. I remember a debate I had as a younger Christian with an older Christian friend who told me that if in Luke 10 (the story of the Good Samaritan) Jesus was not reporting a real robbery on the road from Jerusalem to Jericho and then using it to draw a moral lesson, this friend would cease to believe. I was puzzled and asked why. He said that if Jesus was the divine Son of God, he would not tell truth through a lie. I replied that Luke 10 was a parable, but to no avail.

In addition, biblical truth claims need to be located in their contexts with an appreciation of their place in redemptive history as it unfolds along the biblical plotline. To account for these contexts is to practice what some call "the theological interpretation of Scripture" or, as I understand it, "biblical theology." Brian Rosner brings both these phrases together in this helpful explanation:

> To sum up, biblical theology may be defined as theological interpretation of Scripture in and for the church. It proceeds

---

23. Sproul, *Knowing Scripture*, 58.
24. Sproul, *Knowing Scripture*, 58.

with historical and literary sensitivity and seeks to analyze and synthesize the Bible's teaching about God and his relations to the world on its own terms, maintaining sight of the Bible's overarching narrative and Christocentric focus.[25]

Jesus was the interpreter of the biblical text par excellence. Importantly, he interpreted Scripture theologically. This can be seen vividly in his dialogue with the devil in the wilderness. In Matthew 4:1–11 we see Jesus as the anointed Messiah, bearer of the Spirit, confronted by the tempter. At the end of the encounter Jesus is triumphant. Unlike that other son of God, Israel, which failed in the wilderness when temptation came, this Son of God stays faithful. The first temptation concerns Jesus's hunger. Surely the Son of God can turn stones into bread. Jesus meets the temptation with the word of God (Matt. 4:4; cf. Deut. 8:3):

It is written,

> "Man shall not live by bread alone,
>   but by every word that comes from the mouth
>   of God."

The second temptation uses Scripture. The devil quotes from Psalm 91:11–12, but again Jesus replies with Scripture: "Again it is written, 'You shall not put the Lord your God to the test'" (Matt. 4:7; cf. Deut. 6:16). The last temptation too is met with Scripture (Matt. 4:10; cf. Deut. 6:13):

For it is written,

> "You shall worship the Lord your God
>   and him only shall you serve."

---

25. Brian S. Rosner, "Biblical Theology," in *New Dictionary of Biblical Theology: Exploring the Unity and Diversity of Scripture*, ed. Brian S. Rosner, T. Alexander, Graeme Goldsworthy, and D. A. Carson (Downers Grove, IL: IVP Academic, 2000), 10.

This is no mere proof-texting on Jesus's part. Each time, he quotes from Moses's farewell address to Israel reported in Deuteronomy. This is no accident. Israel succumbed to each of the temptations in the wilderness. Israel complained about their lack of food (Ex. 16:1–3). Israel put God to the test ten times (Num. 14:20–23) and worshiped the golden calf (Ex. 32). That son of God failed. This Son of God does not. Jesus lives by "It is written." But "it is written" is deployed theologically. Each quote is predicated on the contrast between God's Old Testament son and Jesus as the one who is all that Israel should have been.

An Important Distinction

There is an important distinction to be made between one's espoused theology and one's operational theology. We may espouse a high view of Scripture, but our practices may suggest otherwise. For example, if we claim that Scripture is our touchstone but never refer to it in making doctrinal claims, then there is a radical disconnect between what is espoused and what is practiced. Surely this is a spiritually dangerous position to be in.

Scripture does need to be read for its sense. Doctrine needs to be grounded on Scripture, but so does the reader. Scripture needs also to be read for spiritual sustenance. Jesus compared Scripture to bread (Matt. 4). Peter described the word of God as milk (1 Pet. 2:2). Theologian J. I. Packer helps us here in explaining how to do biblical mediation: "Turn what you read about God into prayer and praise to God."[26] The book of Psalms illuminates the way from the very first psalm. Psalm 1 contrasts the righteous person and the wicked one. The righteous person meditates on the instruction of God (*torah*). Psalm 77 puts a finer point on it. The psalmist meditates on the mighty deeds of God. The psalm does not elaborate, but those deeds most likely

---

26. J. I. Packer, *Knowing God* (London: Hodder and Stoughton, 1973), 18–19.

are those of the great rescue of God's people from Egypt and his bringing them into the land of promise—in other words, the gospel of the Old Testament. The Hebrew word for "meditate" in both Psalm 1 and Psalm 77 is used in Isaiah for the sound of doves cooing or moaning (e.g., Isa. 38:14). So, again, most likely it involves a slow, out-loud reading of the text that requires a focused attention. No speed-reading here.

If Scripture is going to feed us and indeed transform us, then it needs to be engaged with our openness to being transformed by it so that what we espouse as Christians and how we operate as Christians are in the closest of connections.

Wisdom from the Past

Metaphor embodies a comparison. A striking metaphor shows the hidden likeness between things now brought out into the open. Sixteenth-century Reformer John Calvin provides three such striking metaphors when it comes to Scripture: Scripture as *spectacles*, Scripture as the *labyrinthine thread*, and Scripture as a *school*. He also provides another striking metaphor in arguing that Scripture is to be read for its *sacra doctrina* (sacred teaching), which constitutes the *scepter* by which Christ rules his church. All these ideas are found in Calvin's famous work *The Institutes of the Christian Religion* of 1559.

As someone who has worn glasses for most of my life, I appreciate Calvin's spectacles metaphor for Scripture. He wrote:

> For as the aged, or those whose sight is defective, when any book however fair, is set before them, though they perceive that there is something written, are scarcely able to make out two consecutive words, but, when aided by glasses, begin to read distinctly, so Scripture, gathering together the impressions of Deity, which, till then, lay

confused in our minds, dissipates the darkness, and shows us the true God clearly.[27]

Scripture brings the character, will, and ways of God into sharp relief. It does the same for understanding humankind. According to Calvin, wisdom lies in knowing God and knowing ourselves. Scripture names the God to whom I pray. I am not like those Athenians whom Paul preached to in Acts 17, who had built an altar to the unknown God. God has spoken. Scripture reveals that I am not the product of blind evolutionary forces or pitiless nature but am made in the image of God (Gen. 1:26–28).

Calvin's next metaphor shows his classical education.

We should consider that the brightness of the Divine countenance, which even an apostle declares to be inaccessible, (1 Tim. 6:16) is a kind of labyrinth,—a labyrinth to us inextricable, if the Word do not serve us as a thread to guide our path; and that it is better to limp in the way, than run with the greatest swiftness out of it.[28]

The Labyrinth was an underground maze in Crete in which King Minos housed a monster.[29] The Minotaur was a hybrid that was both human and bull. Theseus of Athens killed the beast in the Labyrinth and was able to find his way out because Ariadne the daughter of Minos had given him a ball of twine so he could find his way out. (This is a love story too, at least for Ariadne.) The twine became known as the Labyrinthine thread. Calvin's point is that as folk lost in our sin, we need a way back to God. That way is found in Scripture.

---

27. John Calvin, *Institutes of the Christian Religion*, trans. Henry Beveridge, 1.6.1, http://www.ccel.org/ccel/calvin/institutes, accessed June 5, 2019.

28. Calvin, *Institutes*, 1.6.3.

29. For the details of the story, see Simon Goldhill, "Greece," in *World Mythology: The Illustrated Guide*, ed. Roy Willis (Oxford: Oxford University Press, 2006), 150–51.

The apostle Paul construed Scripture as a teacher that instructs (2 Tim. 3:14–17). Calvin's next metaphor is a related one. He saw Scripture as a school in which the believer learns from the Holy Spirit.

> There are others who, when they would cure this disease, recommend that the subject of predestination should scarcely if ever be mentioned, and tell us to shun every question concerning it as we would a rock. Although their moderation is justly commendable in thinking that such mysteries should be treated with moderation, yet because they keep too far within the proper measure, they have little influence over the human mind, which does not readily allow itself to be curbed. Therefore, in order to keep the legitimate course in this matter, we must return to the word of God, in which we are furnished with the right rule of understanding. For Scripture is the school of the Holy Spirit, in which as nothing useful and necessary to be known has been omitted, so nothing is taught but what it is of importance to know.[30]

One last metaphor is worth our attention. In his prefatory address to Francis the king of France, Calvin refers to the word of God as God's scepter. He wrote: "He, moreover, deceives himself who anticipates long prosperity to any kingdom which is not ruled by the scepter of God, that is, by his divine word. For the heavenly oracle is infallible which has declared, that 'where there is no vision the people perish' (Proverbs 29:18)."[31]

The Doctrine of the Trinity: A Textless Doctrine?

The word of God then is our source of the knowledge of God, the definitive witness to the words and deeds of God, and the

---

30. Calvin, *Institutes*, 3.21.3.
31. Calvin, preface to the *Institutes*, 1:15.

norm for both our thinking about God and our living before God. But who is this God we are to believe? And what if the words we use to describe the God of the Bible are not in the Bible? The term "Trinity" is the great example. How do we do faithful theology in this instance? Let's explore the question.

Classic Christianity claims that the one God is Father, Son, and Holy Spirit: one substance in three persons. This is the doctrine of the Holy Trinity. But why believe it? In brief, because of the cumulative weight of many and varied biblical testimonies. That there is only one God is affirmed in both the Old Testament and the New. At the heart of Israel's faith is the claim found in Deuteronomy 6:4–5: "Hear, O Israel: The LORD our God, the LORD is one. You shall love the LORD your God with all your heart and with all your soul and with all your might." Jesus reaffirmed that very claim in debate with the Pharisees in Mark 12:29–30: When asked which commandment matters most, he answered, "The most important is, 'Hear, O Israel: The Lord our God, the Lord is one. And you shall love the Lord your God with all your heart and with all your soul and with all your mind and with all your strength.'"

When the fullness of time came and the Son of God was sent to redeem his people, and when the risen Son poured out the promised Holy Spirit, the idea of oneness soon showed a need for nuancing. Hence, we find that the baptismal formula at the climax of Matthew's account of Jesus affirms both the oneness of the only God there is and the distinctness and inseparability of the Father, the Son, and the Holy Spirit (Matt. 28:18–20):

> And Jesus came and said to them, "All authority in heaven and on earth has been given to me. Go therefore and make disciples of all nations, baptizing them in the name [singular] of the Father and of the Son and of the Holy Spirit,

teaching them to observe all that I have commanded you. And behold, I am with you always, to the end of the age."

These and many other testimonies in the end demanded nothing less than the concept of the Trinity to make sense of them: oneness, threeness, substance, persons, inseparability, and distinctness. My point is a simple one: The doctrine of the Trinity is not a textless doctrine. If it were, and given that Scripture is the *norma normans*, then the doctrine of the Trinity would be fatally wounded.

More Wisdom from the Past

Thomas Cranmer (1489–1556) was the first Protestant archbishop of Canterbury. He was also martyred for his Reformation faith. In fact, there is a mosaic cross set in the Broad Street pavement in Oxford. It marks the place where he was burned at the stake. He knew the value of Scripture as the means by which God spiritually feeds his children. He also knew the importance of prayer in relation to profiting from Scripture. One of his famous prayers is about this. The English is antiquated but the thrust is clear:

> Blessed Lord, which hast caused all holy Scriptures to be written for our learning; grant us that we may in such wise hear them, read, mark, and inwardly digest them; that by patience and comfort of thy holy word, we may embrace, and ever hold fast the blessed hope of everlasting life, which thou hast given us in our savior Jesus Christ.[32]

Conclusion

Doing theology needs a secure epistemological base. God's word written is that base. Textless theology is free of such

---

32. Quoted in C. Frederick Barbee and Paul F. M. Zahl, *The Collects of Thomas Cranmer* (Grand Rapids, MI: Eerdmans, 2006), 4.

divine moorings. It is also important to recognize that other authorities operate in a theologian's life. The evangelical theologian holds to *sola Scriptura*, not *nuda Scriptura*. Reformation scholar Scott Manetsch explains the difference well:

> Evangelical Christians in North America sometimes misunderstand the Reformation doctrine of *sola Scriptura* to mean that the Bible is the Christian's only theological resource, that it can and should be denuded of its churchly context (hence *nuda Scriptura*). Such an understanding is altogether incorrect.[33]

Theology is not done in a tradition-free or context-free zone. For example, in this chapter, Calvin was drawn upon for helpful extrabiblical metaphors to use of Scripture. In other words, I drew upon the Reformation tradition to illuminate the topic under discussion. More will be said about the appeal to the role of tradition in the next chapter. However, suffice it to say for our present purpose that in any contest between Scripture and tradition, Scripture alone (*sola*) is the final court of appeal. In addition, it is important to recognize that the theologian is an interpreter of Scripture.

Once more, the theologian can find help from the past. The Reformers of the sixteenth century had a high view of biblical authority and a way of interpreting Scripture that recognized its nature as the inspired word of God, rather than as a mere anthology of ideas about God in texts from ancient Israel and the early church. Finally, God uses Scripture not only to inform his people but also to transform them. The practice of biblical meditation as found in the Psalms is a key practice serving that end.

---

33. See Scott M. Manetsch, "Is the Reformation Over? John Calvin, Roman Catholicism, and Contemporary Ecumenical Conversations," *Themelios* 36, no. 2 (2011): 199–200, http://themelios.thegospelcoalition.org/article/is-the-reformation-over-john-calvin-roman-catholicism-and-contemporary-ecum.

2

The Witness of Christian Thought and Practice

Past and Present

I can imagine someone saying that if Scripture is our touchtone, why bother with anything else? Isn't having only a Bible sufficient? After all, did not John Wesley (1703–1791), the famous evangelist, say the following?

> I want to know one thing, the way to heaven—how to land safe on that happy shore. God himself has condescended to teach the way: for this very end he came from heaven. He hath written it down in a book. O give me that book! . . . Let me be *homo unius libri* [a man of one book]. Here then I am, far from the busy ways of men. I sit down alone: only God is here. In his presence I open, I read his Book; for this end, to find the way to heaven.[1]

---

1. John Wesley, preface to his *Standard Sermons*, vol. 1, quoted in Rand Maddox, "How John Wesley Read the Bible," Catalyst (website), http://www.catalystresources.org /how-john-wesley-read-the-bible/, accessed April 18, 2017.

So, the argument might go, let me do theology with just God, the Bible, and me.

There is something naïve about this. The fact is that the English Bible I use has been handed to me from the past.[2] It is the work of others who came before me. Indeed, some churches prefer to use only one English translation of the Bible. This itself is a tradition. Indeed, no one reads Scripture in a vacuum. Handing down something from the past is the essence of tradition. Stephen R. Holmes is right to argue that "there is no escape from the mediation of our faith by the tradition."[3]

The famous quote from Wesley needs explaining, however. In context, Wesley was thinking of the Bible alone as the sure guide to heaven. In other words, he had soteriology in mind. No book compares with the Bible on that score. The historical reality is that Wesley prized the Christian tradition, especially as found in the early church. Wesley scholar Randy Maddox comments:

> Among those outside of his circle of associates whom Wesley sought to include in conference were Christians of earlier generations. He particularly valued the writings of the first three centuries of the church, in both its Eastern (Greek) and Western (Latin) settings. In a published letter to Conyers Middleton, he insisted that consultation with these writings had helped many readers avoid dangerous errors in their interpretation of Scripture, while neglect of these writings could leave one captive to misunderstandings currently reigning.[4]

As already noted, a tradition is a hand-me-down or a hand-me-over, something passed on. Tradition operates in all of our

---

2. The English term "tradition" has behind it the Latin "*tradere*," which means "to hand on or hand over."

3. Stephen R. Holmes, *Listening to the Past: The Place of Tradition in Theology* (Grand Rapids, MI: Baker Academic, 2002), 7.

4. Maddox, "How John Wesley Read the Bible."

lives. We have family traditions, church traditions, sporting club traditions, and national traditions, to name a few. I remember vividly the first baseball game I attended in the United States. It was in San Diego, and when the seventh inning came, everyone stood up and started to sing. As an Australian, I was puzzled when we sang, "Take me out to the ballgame," because we were already there. Still, it was and is a noble tradition.

God's people have traditions too. Our great interest is especially in those traditions that have arisen as the people of God have wrestled with the Scriptures over the centuries in the light of this or that pressing concern. Doing theology wisely means learning from the past both positively and negatively.[5] However, in theology tradition can only ever be a *norma normata* (a ruled norm). Again, in a contest between Scripture and tradition, Scripture constitutes the final court of appeal in an evangelical methodology. Even so, it is theological foolishness to ignore the witness of Christian thought and practice—that is, tradition. The Dutch theologian Herman Bavinck (1854–1921) captured the significance of tradition and its relation to Scripture this way: "Tradition in its proper sense is the interpretation and application of the eternal truth in the vernacular and life of the present generation. Scripture without such a tradition is impossible."[6]

Tradition in the Biblical Witness: The Bad and the Good

In chapter 1, I claimed that the appeal to Scripture is fundamental to the evangelical way of doing theology. On any given subject, a useful question to ask is whether Scripture throws light on it. Importantly, Scripture does throw light on tradition.

---

5. For a spirited defense of listening to the past and the need for historical theology, see Holmes, *Listening to the Past*, especially chap. 1.

6. Herman Bavinck, *Reformed Dogmatics*, ed. John Bolt, trans. John Vriend, vol. 1, *Prolegomena* (Grand Rapids, MI: Baker Academic, 2003), 493.

We find in the scriptural testimony that a given tradition can be either bad or good for the people of God. Let's look at examples of each, beginning with the negative.

Tradition as Negative

To elevate tradition over Scripture was the error of the Pharisees, as Mark 7:1–13 shows. Pharisees and some scribes from Jerusalem observed that Jesus's disciples did not eat with washed hands. The tradition of the elders required the washing of hands. On that basis Jesus was asked to please explain: "And the Pharisees and the scribes asked him, 'Why do your disciples not walk according to the tradition of the elders, but eat with defiled hands?'" (v. 5). Jesus was not amused and countered with a quotation from the prophet Isaiah:

> This people honors me with their lips,
> > but their heart is far from me;
> in vain do they worship me,
> > teaching as doctrines the commandments of men.
> > > (Mark 7:6–7; from Isa. 29:13)

Why did he push back? He did so because one of the traditions of the elders was being used to subvert the revealed will of God: namely, the commandment in the Torah itself to honor one's father and mother (Mark 7:9–13).[7] To get around the commandment, a man would simply declare that all he had was Corban (given over to God). That way he could use it throughout his lifetime and not have to part with any of it to support his par-

---

7. The traditions of the elders were developed after the Babylonian exile and Maccabean revolt. They were prescriptions stricter than the Mosaic law. The rationale behind the traditions was that if these prescriptions were followed, then a fence around the Mosaic law was created. By scrupulously observing these non-Torah traditions, the Jew was presumably in no danger of breaking God's law. For an account, see Kenneth D. Litwak, "Traditions of the Elders," in *The New Interpreter's Dictionary of the Bible*, ed. Katharine Doob Sakenfeld, vol. 5, S-Z (Nashville: Abingdon, 2009), 648–49.

ents. Jesus condemned this practice and the reason behind it: "[You are] making void the word of God by your tradition that you have handed down" (v. 13).[8] Jesus summed up the issue in unmistakable terms: "You leave the commandment of God and hold to the tradition of men" (v. 8).

Clearly, traditions can grow up among God's people that undermine the teaching of the Scriptures and harm the health of the church. However, some traditions are worth embracing and vital to the health of the church.

Tradition as Positive

The apostle Paul provides a prime example of a good tradition he embraced and passed on to others. It seems that some at Corinth had problems with the doctrine of the resurrection, so Paul defended it by mounting a cumulative argument in its favor. He wrote, "For I delivered to you as of first importance what I also received: that Christ died for our sins in accordance with the Scriptures, that he was buried, that he was raised on the third day in accordance with the Scriptures, and that he appeared to Cephas, then to the twelve" (1 Cor. 15:3–5).

The language of receiving and delivering is the language of tradition and its transmission. The tradition in view concerns a Christ-centered reading of the Old Testament ("the Scriptures"), which focuses on Jesus's death and resurrection. Importantly, his death is theologically interpreted: "Christ died for our sins." An appeal to historical fact is also part of the tradition: "he appeared to Cephas, then to the twelve." That is not the end of the argument. Paul adds more historical evidence: "Then he appeared to more than five hundred brothers at one time, most of whom are still alive, though some have fallen asleep. Then

---

8. It is worth noting in passing that this New Testament passage clearly shows that the word of God can be in written form. Mostly in the New Testament, "word" or "word of God" language refers to the preached gospel (e.g., 1 Pet. 1:22–25).

he appeared to James, then to all the apostles" (15:6–7). The apostle is not finished. Next comes his own experience: "Last of all, as to one untimely born, he appeared also to me" (15:8). Yet there is one more strand of argument. Paul shows the logic of the alternative through a number of hypothetical "if . . . then" statements. For example, if Christ is not risen, what follows is hopeless despair (15:12–19). In this light, Paul can then confidently affirm, "But in fact Christ has been raised from the dead, the firstfruits of those who have fallen asleep" (15:20).

So from our New Testament we learn that some traditions are to be embraced and others rejected. Discernment is crucial. The subsequent history of the church reveals the same need for discernment.

Tradition in Christian Thought and Practice: The Bad and the Good

A knowledge of the New Testament would alert us to the fact that the traditions found in church history and tools for theological thought generated in the course of church history will likewise be a mix of the healthy and the unhealthy, even toxic. An early church controversy and an insight from B. B. Warfield will serve as illustrations.

Learning from the Fathers: The Arian Controversy

In the church I attend, every week we recite the Nicene Creed of the late fourth century in response to hearing the Bible read publicly and preached.[9] The idea is that having heard the word of God read and explained, we respond in faith. A key state-

---

9. Strictly speaking, the Nicene Creed is the Niceno-Constantinopolitan Creed of AD 381 with the Western addition confessing that the Spirit proceeds from both the Father and the Son. The addition dates from the sixth century. This later creed incorporates the earlier Nicene Creed of AD 325 with its affirmation of the deity of the Son but makes it clearer that the Spirit too is to be worshiped and glorified along with the Father and the Son. In other words, the 381 creed affirms the deity of the Spirit against the backdrop of some in the late fourth-century church who were denying it.

ment in that creed declares regarding Jesus, "We believe in one Lord, Jesus Christ, the only Son of God, eternally begotten of the Father, God from God, Light from Light, true God from true God, begotten not made, of one being with the Father." The phrase "of one being with the Father" has generated enormous discussion and debate over the centuries. The issue it raises concerns the relation of the Father and the Son, and that is not a dead issue. For example, both the Jehovah's Witness and the Muslim would find its claim impossible to embrace (more on this later).

The Nicene Creed of AD 325 was born out of theological controversy over the theological views of Arius, a presbyter in the church in Alexandria, who around 318 took issue with his bishop's understanding of the relation between the Father and the Son.[10] The debate was no minor one. Historian Mark A. Noll describes it as one of the key "turning points" in the history of Christianity.[11]

Exploring the issue raised by the ancient creed requires some historical understanding. Put another way, we need to delve into the witness of Christian thought and practice. It was Emperor Constantine himself who called the Council of Nicaea into being in 325. The key doctrinal issue was the relation of the Father to the Son. Arius taught that there was a time when the Son was not. In other words, the Son did not stand on the same ontological ground as the Father. The Son was a creature, albeit the highest of creatures. Alexandria in Egypt was one of the great cities of the empire, and the emperor needed a unified empire and church after years of civil

---

10. The definitive work on fourth-century Arianism is that of Lewis Ayres, *Nicaea and Its Legacy: An Approach to Fourth-Century Trinitarian Theology* (Oxford: Oxford University Press, 2006).

11. Mark A. Noll, *Turning Points: Decisive Moments in the History of Christianity*, 2nd ed. (Grand Rapids, MI: Baker Academic, 2000), 47–64. For a fine account of the theological issues involved and the history of the debate, see Frances M. Young, *From Nicaea to Chalcedon*, 2nd ed. (Grand Rapids, MI: Baker Academic, 2010), 42–56.

war and strife. And here was a presbyter, Arius, in conflict with his bishop, Alexander.

Arius had a knack for communication. He put his theology into memorable poetry (set to drinking-song tunes). In fact, at the Council of Nicaea, Arius sang to the emperor:

> The uncreated God has made the Son
> A beginning of things created,
> And by adoption has God made the Son
> Into an advancement of himself.
> Yet the Son's substance is
> Removed from the substance of the Father:
> The Son is not equal to the Father,
> Nor does he share the same substance.
> God is the all-wise Father,
> And the Son is the teacher of his mysteries.
> The members of the Holy Trinity
> Share unequal glories.[12]

If this theology were true, then any worship of Christ would be idolatry. A good question to ask of any theology is, Assuming it is true, what may I expect to find or not expect to find in the New Testament witness? If Arianism were true, I would not expect Jesus to be the object of worship in the New Testament, but he is (see Rev. 5:11–14, for example).[13]

The council, composed of over two hundred bishops and with the emperor in attendance, rejected the Arian stance and instead affirmed: "We believe in one God, the Father Almighty, Maker of all things visible and invisible. And in one Lord Jesus Christ, the Son of God, begotten not made, being of one sub-

---

12. Quoted in Noll, *Turning Points*, 53.
13. Alan Richardson, *Creeds in the Making: A Short Introduction to the History of Christian Doctrine* (London: SCM, 1972), 53, also notes that if Arianism is true, then the worship of Jesus is idolatry. He adds three other corollaries: there is no incarnation; an unknowable God cannot be revealed by a mere creature; and only God can redeem—a lesser being cannot.

stance [Greek, *homoousios*] with the Father; by whom all things were made."[14] This contradicted Arius's doctrine at a number of points. Jesus is begotten, not made. Jesus is one being with the Father—distinct from the Father, yes; less than God, no. The term *homoousios* is not in the Bible and met with criticism after the council.[15] Why use a term not found in the Bible? To this question we now turn.

Learning from the Moderns: A Tool for Thought

I have a toolbox at home. For some tasks I need a screwdriver. For others I need a clamp. For still others I need my phone because I am out of my depth and should call in an expert. These are physical objects. But there are other sorts of tools. These tools you cannot handle, but you can think with them. They are conceptual tools.

When it comes to Trinitarian thought, B. B. Warfield (1851–1921) provides an excellent tool in making a distinction between words and their sense. What do I mean? Warfield tackled a long-standing question about the use of the term "Trinity."[16] How can a word not in the Bible be used justifiably in referring to the God of the Bible? In a classic essay, Warfield argues:

> The term "Trinity" is not a Biblical term, and we are not using Biblical language when we define what is expressed by it as the doctrine that there is one only and true God, but in the unity of the Godhead there are three coeternal and coequal Persons, the same in substance but distinct

---

14. Richardson, *Creeds in the Making*, 57.

15. According to Lewis Ayres, generally speaking the term *homoousios* went into eclipse during the years 326–350. See Ayres, *Nicaea and Its Legacy*, 431. It was from the 360s on that a "pro-Nicene group clearly emerge[d]" (434). The Council of Constantinople in 381 solidified the use of *homoousios* as well as the idea of the deity of the Holy Spirit, who, with the Father and the Son, is to be worshiped and glorified.

16. Tertullian was the first to use the term *trinitas* (Latin). See J. N. D. Kelly, *Early Christian Doctrines*, 5th ed. (London: Adam and Charles Black, 1977), 113.

in subsistence. A doctrine so defined can be spoken of as a Biblical doctrine only on the principle that the sense of Scripture is Scripture. And the definition of a Biblical doctrine in such un-Biblical language can be justified only on the principle that it is better to preserve the truth of Scripture than the words of Scripture.[17]

Warfield offers great theological and philosophical wisdom. His argument about the term "Trinity" applies also to the use of the Greek term *homoousios* (being of one substance) in the Nicene Creed. Sense and terminology need to be distinguished. The sense of biblical teaching is often captured in terminology from outside the biblical text. If that were not so, then translations of the Bible into languages other than the original Hebrew, Aramaic, and Koine Greek would be folly.[18]

I have learned from Warfield and have passed on his tool to generations of theological students.

A Dead Issue?

Why bother with a fourth-century debate about the nature of God? We bother because theologians in that century needed to wrestle with the question of the relation of the Father to the Son in a way that the New Testament writers did not need to. But with the challenge posed by the Jehovah's Witnesses and the rise of Islam, we also need to. In other words, we can learn from the fathers, the tradition.

The Jehovah's Witnesses reject the doctrine of the Trinity as lacking any biblical basis. Furthermore, they argue: "Many Christian denominations teach that God is a Trinity. However,

---

17. B. B. Warfield, *Biblical Foundations* (London: Tyndale Press, 1958), 79.

18. In fact, numerous theological terms are not found in the Bible: for example, "Christology," "Pneumatology," and "penal substitution." However, these English terms represent master concepts backed by numerous biblical testimonies and provide a shorthand way of speaking of them.

note what the *Encyclopædia Britannica* states: 'Neither the word "Trinity" nor the explicit doctrine appears in the New Testament. . . . The doctrine developed gradually over several centuries and through many controversies.'"[19] Here, as with fourth-century Arians, the absence of a term from the Bible is considered problematic.[20] This is where Warfield's insight about a term and its sense is of such help. The term may not be in the Bible ("Trinity," *homoousios*), but the idea is.

Regarding Islam, early church fathers such as John of Damascus (676–749) certainly believed that Muhammad was in part informed by Arianism. The Damascene wrote: "From that time to the present a false prophet named Mohammed has appeared in their midst. This man, after having chanced upon the Old and New Testaments and likewise, it seems, having conversed with an Arian monk, devised his own heresy."[21]

Given the way many Christians pray these days, one might be forgiven for thinking that the idea of God as Trinity is a dead one and that Muslims and Christians worship the same God. How many times I have heard prayers like this in churches: "Dear God, bless so and so and help so and so. . . . Amen." There is no mention of the Father or the Son, let alone the Holy Spirit. It is Unitarian praying. So when the Muslim argues that the Christian and Muslim worship the same God, there seems to be no obvious difference.

---

19. "Is God a Trinity?," JW.org, https://www.jw.org/en/bible-teachings/questions/trinity/, accessed April 28, 2017.

20. Interestingly, the Jehovah's Witnesses know of Arius and his dissent from Athanasian theology. See "Called Out of Darkness," JW.org, https://www.jw.org/en/publications/magazines/watchtower-study-november-2016/called-out-of-darkness/, accessed May 1, 2017.

21. The quote is from John of Damascus, *Fount of Knowledge*, pt. 2, in "St. John of Damascus's Critique of Islam," Orthodox Christian Information Center (website), http://orthodoxinfo.com/general/stjohn_islam.aspx, accessed May 1, 2017. Marco Michelis, "John of Damascus," in *Muhammad in History, Thought and Culture: An Encyclopedia of the Prophet of God*, ed. Coeli Fitzpatrick and Adam Hani Walker (Santa Barbara, CA: ABC-Clio, 2014), 327, argues, "The question of Arian influence on early Islam is worthy of further inquiry."

But there is a massive difference. Trinitarian praying, to the Muslim, is an exercise in idolatry. The idea of the triune God is incoherent and irrational to Islam.[22] However, the genius of New Testament praying to the Father in the name of the Son in reliance on the Holy Spirit is that it structures the gospel of Christ the mediator into Christian praying.

Some Wise Words on *Sola Scriptura*

Scott Manetsch's distinction between *sola Scriptura* and *nuda Scriptura* is worth revisiting at this juncture:

> Evangelical Christians in North America sometimes misunderstand the Reformation doctrine of *sola Scriptura* to mean that the Bible is the Christian's only theological resource, that it can and should be denuded of its churchly context (hence *nuda Scriptura*). Such an understanding is altogether incorrect.
>
> Calvin believed that Holy Scripture as the only infallible rule of faith and practice should serve as the final authority by which to judge Christian doctrine and practice, but it was not his only resource for theology. Consequently, he regularly consulted and appealed to early Christian documents and church authorities—most notably Augustine—to gain theological insight and clarity on contested doctrinal matters. He recognized the strategic importance of demonstrating the continuity of Protestant teaching with the core convictions of the early Church. Thus, his regular refrain: "The ancient church is on our side!"

---

22. See, for example, Shabbir Akhtar, *Islam as Political Religion: The Future of an Imperial Faith* (London and New York: Routledge, 2011), 162–65. Akhtar is an Oxford-trained analytical philosopher, and so it is disappointing to find such a facile analysis in his work on this matter, as the sources he draws on shows. He would have been better served by consulting a book such as Tarmo Toom, *Classical Trinitarian Theology: A Textbook* (London: T&T Clark, 2007). That way I might have recognized the Trinity he rejects.

In a similar fashion, evangelical Protestants should view the riches of the Christian tradition(s) during and before the sixteenth-century Reformation not simply as an "alien world" or as an unfortunate parenthesis. Instead, they should view them as an important resource for biblical interpretation, theological reflection, and ecumenical dialogue while at the same time insisting that everything be tested carefully by the authoritative Word of God.[23]

Manetsch is right in arguing that Christians should look to resources from the past and can draw on them in the present without undermining the idea of *sola Scriptura*. He is also right to insist that "everything be tested carefully by the authoritative Word of God." This is another important principle handed down from the past: namely, the idea of *semper reformanda* (always reforming).

Conclusion

Theological thinking involves historical thinking. The theologian has behind him or her the great stream of Christian thought and practice.[24] We are not the first generation to follow Christ. Responsible theological thinking takes this into account. We all stand in a tradition of Christian thought and practice. It is important that we are aware of this fact. In practice, this means that whatever tradition we stand in needs to be open to reform by the word of God. This is because Scripture, as I have argued, is the ruling norm (*norma normans*), while tradition is a ruled

---

23. See Scott M. Manetsch, "Is the Reformation Over? John Calvin, Roman Catholicism, and Contemporary Ecumenical Conversations," *Themelios* 36, no. 2 (2011): 199–200, http://themelios.thegospelcoalition.org/article/is-the-reformation-over-john-calvin-roman-catholicism-and-contemporary-ecum.

24. See Graham A. Cole, "Thinking Theologically," *Reformed Theological Review* 48, no. 2 (1989): 52. I myself stand in the tradition of Reformation Anglicanism, with luminaries such as Thomas Cranmer (1489–1556), George Whitefield (1714–1770), Charles Simeon (1759–1836), J. C. Ryle (1816–1900), John Stott (1921–2011), and J. I. Packer (1926–).

norm (*norma normata*). We need Scripture to be the final court of appeal because, as we have seen, there are healthy traditions and unhealthy, even toxic, ones for the life of the church.

An intentional openness on our parts to the reforming power of Scripture may also help us escape traditionalism as described in this helpful distinction by Jaroslav Pelikan: "Tradition is the living faith of the dead; traditionalism is the dead faith of the living."[25] The Nicene tradition served as a healthy example, and Arianism, an unhealthy one. Ideas have consequences, and as philosopher George Santayana famously said: "Those who cannot remember the past are condemned to repeat it."[26]

---

25. Jaroslav Pelikan, *The Vindication of Tradition: The 1983 Jefferson Lecture in Humanities* (New Haven, CT: Yale University Press, 1984), 65. It is instructive to see in Timothy Keller's fine book on prayer how he not only draws on Scripture but turns to Augustine, Luther, and Calvin for "master classes" (his phrase) in prayer. In other words, he values both the normative Scriptures (supremely) and the witness of Christian thought and practice. Keller, *Prayer: Experiencing Awe and Intimacy with God* (New York: Penguin, 2014), chaps. 6–7.

26. George Santayana, *The Life of Reason, or, The Phases of Human Progress*, critical ed., ed. Marianne S. Wokeck and Martin A. Coleman (Cambridge, MA: MIT Press, 2011), 172.

3

The World of Human Brokenness

As I write this chapter, I am looking out on beautiful green woods and sunlight breaking through leaves. I know where I am. I am in my office on campus. I know the suburb in which the campus is placed, the big city near which the suburb is found, the state in which the city is located, the country in which the state located, and the hemisphere. And I know the time of year. It is spring. I know the day, the month, and the year. In fact, all I need to do is look at the bottom right-hand corner of my computer, and there is the time and the date.

I am also conscious that things aren't the way they are supposed to be.[1] There is war in the Middle East, and the threat of terrorism is a daily concern somewhere in the world. Rogue nations have increasing nuclear weapon capability. Poverty on the African continent still stalks so much of the landmass. There are concerns about pollution and global warming. South of

---

1. See Cornelius Plantinga, *Not the Way It's Supposed to Be: A Breviary of Sin* (Grand Rapids, MI: Eerdmans, 1996).

where I am living there is ongoing gang violence. Fifty shootings over a weekend no longer are a surprise. Innocents are killed in cross fire. Racial hatred seems to be growing. The world in which I am placed seems so broken. The humanist confidence in the power of education to change human nature for the better seems to be a failing project.

However, there is another way to understand space and time. There is another explanation for the brokenness of the world. This other way is crucial if we are to understand our context rightly. This other explanation is vital if we are to avoid romanticism, which is naive about human nature, as well as numbing pessimism, which is cynical about human nature.

The Fractures of the Fall

In the light of the biblical revelation, doing theology acknowledges the setting in which the task takes place and also the era in which doing theology is done. We live in the new normal, or abnormal, given the fall (as Augustine taught) or the rupture (as Jacques Ellul suggested) delineated in Genesis 3. Put another way, we live outside Eden, outside of paradise. This is our experience. It is a world of brokenness. Doing theology is concerned with engaging the context in which we actually live, not a theoretical one, and this brings us to this idea of the new normal.

The New Normal

As a kid I watched black-and-white television and used a dial phone. Now I watch television in colorful HD, and my phone is sometimes smarter than I am. Change happens. An old normal can give way to a new one. So too in the Bible's presentation of human history. Genesis 1–2 presents a creation in harmony with God. The apex of creatures is humankind created to image God (Gen. 1:26–28). The purpose of this image is to represent the living God by relating to him and exercising godlike functions. We see in Genesis 2 Adam exercising care and control over the garden environment. He names other creatures, just like God did in the first chapter of Genesis. However, Adam is alone, and so another like him, yet different from him, is fashioned. Then, suddenly, peace is shattered by the intrusion of the serpent and our first parents' succumbing to temptation in Genesis 3. There is now a new normal. The relation between God and his images is ruptured; so too is the relation between the images (male and female), within the image (the sense of shame), and with the environment ("thorns and thistles," v. 18). In Genesis 3, there is no room for a facile romanticism about the perfectibility of human nature. But given the promise of a divine intervention in verse 15—the overthrow of the serpent—there is no room for cynical pessimism about the human story.

The apostle Paul elaborates on this new normal in Romans 1–3. He concludes this part of his argument with the claim that "all have sinned and fall short of the glory of God" (3:23). In Paul's view, all of humankind now stands guilty before God and is the object of his judicial anger (wrath). Given the fall, the believer should always be disappointed by destructive human behavior, but never surprised. Humankind is out of moral step with the Creator.

The Groaning Creation and the Present Age

Various scientific theories foresee a bleak future of the natural order. For example, the Big Freeze theory contends that the universe will keep expanding and consequently get colder and colder. Maximal entropy will be reached. The Big Rip theory also posits an expanding universe. Matter cannot hold together and will rip apart, whether stars or subatomic particles. The Big Crunch theory maintains that expansion will end and the universe will collapse into itself until a black-hole-like singularity is all there is.

Over a hundred years ago, Bertrand Russell, the famous unbeliever of the last century, wrote "A Free Man's Worship" in 1903. He based his argument on the science of his day, but given the Big Freeze, the Big Rip, and the Big Crunch scenarios, his pessimism remains persuasive.

> Such, in outline, but even more purposeless, more void of meaning, is the world which Science presents for our belief. Amid such a world, if anywhere, our ideals henceforward must find a home. That Man is the product of causes which had no prevision of the end they were achieving; that his origin, his growth, his hopes and fears, his loves and his beliefs, are but the outcome of accidental collocations of atoms; that no fire, no heroism, no intensity of thought and feeling, can preserve an individual life beyond the grave; that all the labours of the ages, all the devotion, all the inspiration, all the noonday brightness of human genius, are destined to extinction in the vast death of the solar system, and that the whole temple of Man's achievement must inevitably be buried beneath the debris of a universe in ruins—all these things, if not quite beyond dispute, are yet so nearly certain, that no philosophy which rejects them can hope to stand.[2]

Russell concluded, "Only within the scaffolding of these truths, only on the firm foundation of unyielding despair, can the soul's habitation henceforth be safely built."[3]

In contrast to these dark scenarios, according to Saint Paul we live in a "groaning" creation awaiting its liberation. Failure to take this setting seriously leads to foolish, not wise, theol-

---

2. See Bertrand Russell, *A Free Man's Worship*, http://www.skeptic.ca/Bertrand_Russell_Collection.pdf, accessed October 17, 2017.

3. Russell, *A Free Man's Worship*.

ogy. In Romans 8, Paul makes a remarkable comparison: "For I consider that the sufferings of this present time are not worth comparing with the glory that is to be revealed to us" (v. 18). Paul's rationale comes next: "For the creation waits with eager longing for the revealing of the sons of God" (v. 19). Human destiny and the universe's destiny are tied together, but not just any humans are in view. This hoped-for destiny is for those who are now part of the family of God, and glory awaits: "For the creation was subjected to futility, not willingly, but because of him who subjected it, in hope that the creation itself will be set free from its bondage to corruption and obtain the freedom of the glory of the children of God" (vv. 20–21). Paul makes a striking point: "For we know that the whole creation has been groaning together in the pains of childbirth until now" (v. 22). This is an amazing hope of sweeping scope. Here is no Platonic dismissal of the worth of the material order. Here is no Gnostic flight from the natural order. Matter has a destiny in the transfigured new heavens and the new earth, to use the language of Isaiah and Revelation. This is a hope worth waiting for patiently (v. 25).

Paul's reference to the created order's need for liberation shows that he takes Genesis 3 and its ramifications seriously. In fact, in his Galatian letter he draws on the idea of two ages— this one and the one to come—to express his realism: "Grace to you and peace from God our Father and the Lord Jesus Christ, who gave himself for our sins to deliver us from the present evil age, according to the will of our God and Father, to whom be the glory forever and ever. Amen" (Gal. 1:3–5).

The Last Days

As for the time frame in which God has placed us, the letter to the Hebrews is instructive. The last days is an expression found in Hebrews 1:1–2: "Long ago, at many times and in many ways, God spoke to our fathers by the prophets, but in these last days he has spoken to us by his Son, whom he appointed the heir of all things, through whom also he created the world." Clearly, revelation is progressive as the writer of the letter draws a comparison between the past ("our fathers") and his present ("the Son"). Revelation through the Son is the climax of a revelatory process, and this is captured in the phrase "the last days." The next great revelatory event is the return of Christ, when he appears a second time (Heb. 9:27).

So, then, in biblical perspective our context for doing theology with respect to space is the groaning creation, and with respect to time is the last days. To the matter of context we now turn.

Context and Questions

Theologian Helmut Thielicke wrote, "Living dogmatics [another term for doctrine] never allows its problems to be self-originated as by a virgin birth, but it is always being fertilized, achieving its productive impulse through the questions of the time."[4] Different contexts have family resemblances and differences. Brokenness will show itself in adultery, theft, and murder. It is hard to think of a society in which any of these three attract no moral blame. However, how the idolatries of the human heart express themselves may differ radically. I have been in pagan temples where the idols are in wood, stone, and precious metals. Most of my life, however, has been lived in the context of Western affluence. Here idolatry is subtler but no less real: the worship of career, pleasure, and wealth.[5]

---

4. Helmut Thielicke, *A Little Exercise for Young Theologians*, trans. Charles L. Taylor (Grand Rapids, MI: Eerdmans, 1978), 28.

5. I will say more about this shortly when I discuss the supernatural opponent of faithful theology.

Transcending Context

Gregory A. Boyd and Paul R. Eddy describe two ways of doing theology. The "traditional evangelical model," in Carl F. Henry's words, is to argue that the "Scriptures contain a body of divinely given information actually expressed or capable of being expressed in propositions."[6] The more recent view is that of the "postfoundationalist model." On this view, says Stanley Grenz, "the categories we employ in our theology are by necessity culturally and historically conditioned, and as theologians each of us is both 'a child of the times' and a communicator to those times."[7] Together with Roger E. Olson, Grenz also wrote: "Our understanding of Scripture will always be filtered through the lenses of who we are and where we are in time and space."[8]

The interesting fact is that Grenz and Olson recognize that they are conditioned by their times. So too am I. However, if we were *wholly* conditioned by our times, would we even know it? If I may use a question posed by C. S. Lewis for my purposes: "Do fish complain of the sea being wet?"[9] Presumably not. Fish do not transcend their watery environment. What needs to be noted is that the human imagination, unlike fish, enables us to transcend our own times and establish a critical distance from them.[10] There is more to be said for the traditional evangelical model than some appear to think.

---

6. Quoted in Gregory A. Boyd and Paul R. Eddy, *Across the Spectrum: Understanding Issues in Evangelical Theology*, 2nd ed. (Grand Rapids, MI: Baker Academic, 2009), 294. Of course, to argue as Henry does is not to imply that propositions are all that is contained in Scripture. The traditional evangelical model can be caricatured, not that Boyd or Eddy offers a caricature.

7. Stanley J. Grenz, *Revisioning Evangelical Theology: A Fresh Agenda for the 21st Century* (Downers Grove, IL: InterVarsity Press, 1993), 83.

8. Stanley J. Grenz and Roger E. Olson, *Who Needs Theology? An Invitation to the Study of God* (Downers Grove, IL: InterVarsity Press, 1996), 90.

9. Quoted in Sheldon Vanauken, *A Severe Mercy: A Story of Faith, Tragedy, and Triumph* (New York: HarperCollins, 1987), 93. Lewis's point is that we complain about time flying, but if materialism were true, why would we?

10. I understand the human imagination is that capacity we have to envisage other possible worlds and from that vantage point critique our real world.

Doing Theology in Between

Another way to look at the context in which we undertake the theological task is to recognize that we do our theology in between the first coming of Christ and his return. For Martin Luther, this meant that he did theology under the cross (a *theologia crucis*) and not as though he were in glory contemplating the face of God (a *theologia gloriae*). One consequence of understanding life between Christ's first and second comings is to be humbled. As James wrote, "Not many of you should become teachers, my brothers, for you know that we who teach will be judged with greater strictness. For we all stumble in many ways. And if anyone does not stumble in what he says, he is a perfect man, able also to bridle his whole body" (3:1–2). Virtues play a role in doing theology, and humility is key. The humble theologian is open to correction and further reform of thought and life. Again, the Reformation slogan *semper reformanda* (always reforming) in the light of God's word is sound. The unteachable theologian is an oxymoron.[11]

Given that we can indeed stumble, it is important that we do our theologizing in fellowship with others. One of the joys of being on a theology faculty is learning from colleagues. For example, I was in conversation with a colleague who was a specialist in the Old Testament. We were talking about Genesis 1. He pointed out that in Genesis 1:2, where the Spirit of God hovers over the waters, the Spirit does not touch the waters. If the Spirit were depicted as touching the water, we would have a text typical of ancient Near Eastern creation myths (e.g., the Babylonian *Enuma Elish*). In those myths, the material order flows

---

11. Kevin J. Vanhoozer, "From Bible to Theology," in *Theology, Church, and Ministry: A Handbook for Theological Education*, ed. David S. Dockery (Nashville: B&H Academic, 2017), is writing about theological education, but what he says applies to doing theology too: "[It] has nothing to do with mastery and everything to do with learning" (242). By definition, a disciple is a learner, and Vanhoozer rightly sees interpreting the Bible "as an aspect of discipleship."

out of the divine order. It is an emanationist worldview. Not so in Genesis 1. In the biblical account of creation, the distinction between the Creator and the creature is never compromised.

Similarly, a different colleague gave me an insight into why a whole animal carcass, including its innards, could be burned up in the Old Testament sacrificial system. In the ancient Near East, animal entrails were used for guidance. In contradistinction, in Israel Yahweh alone guides.

So, then, theologizing in fellowship with others adds wisdom and depth to our theology.

Faithful Theology's Opponent

In a classic work, Harry Blamires outlines the defining characteristics of a Christian mind.[12] He posits six characteristics. The Christian mind has a supernatural orientation: "The Christian mind sees human life and human history held in the hands of God. . . . It sees the natural order as dependent upon the supernatural order, time as contained within eternity."[13] It also has a conception of truth where "Christianity imposes the given divine revelation as the final touchstone of truth."[14] The Christian mind, according to Blamires, accepts the authority of God and acknowledges that the choice is "either the bowed head or the turned back."[15] As well, it sees more value in persons than in machines. Persons are sacred.[16] It has a sacramental cast, which means that the human experience of beauty, for example, can be an intimation of heaven and its glory.[17] But importantly for our purposes, Blamires argues that a sixth defining characteristic of the Christian mind is its awareness

---

12. Harry Blamires, *The Christian Mind* (London: SPCK, 1966).
13. Blamires, *The Christian Mind*, 67.
14. Blamires, *The Christian Mind*, 107.
15. Blamires, *The Christian Mind*, 132.
16. Blamires, *The Christian Mind*, 156.
17. Blamires, *The Christian Mind*, 188.

of evil: "It is conscious of the universe as a battlefield between the forces of good and evil."[18]

Informed by the word of revelation, the believer is aware that God, his word, and his people have an opponent bent on harm. The devil knows how to ask theological questions that impugn the good character of God. Dietrich Bonhoeffer points out that sin enters the human world through a religious question: "Did God say, 'You shall not eat of any tree in the garden'?"[19] According to Bonhoeffer, "The serpent's question was a thoroughly religious one. But with the first religious question in the world, evil has come upon the scene."[20] He elaborates: "What is the real evil in this question? . . . It is that the false answer is contained within it, that within it is attacked the basic attitude of the creature towards the Creator. Man is expected to be the judge of God's word instead of simply hearing and doing it."[21] The evil's aim is "to divert man from the Word of God."[22]

Our theological awareness shows itself in our prayers. The content of our praying reveals what we really believe and value. Evagrius Ponticus (345/46–399) famously said: "If you are a theologian, you will pray truly. And if you pray truly, you are a theologian."[23] Truly praying requires an awareness of reality, and reality in biblical perspective is construed as a drama in which good and evil are presently in conflict. Yet there are many recent and contemporary theologians for whom doing theology does not reckon with supernatural opposition to the word of

---

18. Blamires, *The Christian Mind*, 86.

19. Dietrich Bonhoeffer, *Creation and Fall, Temptation: Two Studies*, trans. John C. Fletcher (New York: Simon and Schuster, 1997), 72.

20. Bonhoeffer, *Creation and Fall, Temptation*, 73.

21. Bonhoeffer, *Creation and Fall, Temptation*, 74.

22. Bonhoeffer, *Creation and Fall, Temptation*, 75.

23. Evagrius Ponticus, "On Prayer," par. 61, The Desert Fathers (blog), http://desert fathers.blogspot.com/2011/06/works-of-evagrius-ponticuson-prayer.html, accessed April 28, 2016.

God. The most famous example is the German New Testament scholar and theologian Rudolf Bultmann (1884–1976) and his demythologizing program in the 1940s. He argued, "We cannot use electric lights and radios and, in the event of illness, avail ourselves of modern medical and clinical means and at the same time believe in the spirit and wonder of the New Testament."[24]

Bultmann exemplifies what missiologist Paul Hiebert (1932–2007) recognized as "the flaw of the excluded middle." A more recent example is provided by the joint work by Miguel A. De La Torre and Albert Hernandez. The subject of their book is Satan, in which they conclude:

> We have ended the quest for the historical Satan by finding him in the mirror. We have seen Satan, and much too often over the past twenty centuries he has been us Christians. The real quest that now lies before us is finding a way to exorcize this Satan and the demonic legions lodged within the heart of and mind of an exclusivist and persecuting tradition.[25]

According to Hiebert, however, many Christians in the West have forgotten that there is another order of intelligent created life playing its role in the drama of salvation. By this he meant the devil and his demonic entourage. He chided himself as a Western-trained theologian:

> The reasons for my uneasiness with the biblical and Indian world views should now be clear. I had excluded the middle level of supernatural but this-worldly beings and

---

24. Rudolf Bultmann, "The New Testament and Mythology: The Problem of Demythologizing the New Testament Proclamation" (1941), in *The New Testament and Mythology and Other Basic Writings*, ed. Schubert Ogden (Philadelphia: Fortress, 1984), 4. For a recent counter to Bultmann's antisupernaturalism, see Craig S. Keener's magisterial study, *Miracles: The Credibility of New Testament Accounts*, 2 vols. (Grand Rapids, MI: Baker Academic, 2011).

25. Miguel A. De La Torre and Albert Hernandez, *The Quest for the Historical Satan* (Minneapolis: Fortress, 2011), 220.

forces from my own world view. As a scientist I had been trained to deal with the empirical world in naturalistic terms. As a theologian, I was taught to answer ultimate questions in theistic terms. For me the middle zone did not really exist. Unlike Indian villagers, I had given little thought to spirits of this world, to local ancestors and ghosts, or to the soul of animals. For me these belonged to the realm of fairies, trolls, and other mythical beings.[26]

The majority world has not fallen for the flaw. Indeed, I contend that this is a dimension of doing theology where Western theologians can learn from the wider world of Christian believing. There are places in the broken world where the devil appears to be active just as Peter described; the "roaring lion" is on the prowl (1 Pet. 5:8). In other parts of our globe, he is disguised as "an angel of light," his modus operandi being through false teachers and teaching (2 Cor. 11:13–15). Therefore, doing theology requires us to be aware of our context between the ages of Christ's first and second comings.

The Trinity and Human Brokenness

Augustine famously wrote: "You move us to delight in praising You; for You have made us for Yourself, and our hearts are restless until they rest in You."[27] Dan Graves rightly contextualizes these famous words:

> Behind Augustine are a succession of desperate searches
> for fulfillment: excessive pleasures, false religions, philoso-
> phy, dissipation and distractions—futilities that left him
> so weary of himself he could only cry out, "How long, O

26. Paul G. Hiebert, *Anthropological Reflections on Missiological Issues* (Grand Rapids, MI: Baker, 1994), 196.

27. Augustine, *The Confessions* 1.1.1, New Advent (website), http://www.newadvent.org/fathers/110101.htm, accessed July 20, 2019.

Lord, how long?" At the very moment when he uttered that cry, circumstances led his eyes to a passage in Romans that showed him he could be freed from sin. Shortly afterward, he was baptized.

Now, a decade since his baptism, after long musing upon the transformation that took place in him when he finally believed, he begins a unique autobiographical and philosophical prayer to God, a book which will become one of the most original and famous works in all of literature, the world's first psychological "autobiography." The Confessions will be his testimony of God's interaction with a soul that has found rest in its Creator.

Heart bursting with the reality of God, he addresses his manuscript directly to the Lord as one long prayer and meditation—a prayer and meditation that will take him five years to complete. He dips his quill and begins, "Great are you, O Lord, and greatly to be praised; great is your power, and your wisdom is infinite."

In contrast to God, he muses, what is man? Yet there is a connection between the two. Humans, such a small part of creation and short-lived as they are, still find a need to praise God. In spite of sin, each feels the longing to reach out to his Creator. Why is this? He realizes it is the doing of God. "You have made us for yourself, and *our hearts are restless, until they can find rest in you.*"

That line summarizes the theme of Augustine's life and will not be bettered in all the writings that lie ahead of him, in which he will wrestle with the deepest issues of theology.[28]

The God whom Augustine addresses is the eternal Trinity, the only God there is.

---

28. Dan Graves, "Our Hearts Are Restless," Christian History Institute (website), article 15, https://christianhistoryinstitute.org/incontext/article/augustine, accessed October 26, 2017; my emphasis. Quoted by permission.

An implication of the reality that God is triune is that relationships are at the heart of reality and always have been. Jesus in his high priestly prayer of John 17 spoke of the love between the Father and him and the glory between them before there was even a creation. It is no surprise, then, that we creatures, made to image God, hunger for relationships. D. Broughton Knox captures the relational significance of the Trinity well:

> Ultimate reality is good, personal, relational. And these relationships are other-person-centered, as all good true relationships must be. This is the character of God and this is how creation has been made. We have been created in God's image for relationship and this relationship must be other-person-centered.[29]

However, the fall has wrought relational havoc. The tragedy is, to quote the song, "lookin' for love in all the wrong places."[30] The good news of the gospel is that redemption is about the restoration of right relationships: to our loving God, with one another, and with the environment of the world to come. Such a restoration is the Christian's hope. As 2 Peter 3:13 says, "According to his promise we are waiting for new heavens and a new earth in which righteousness [right relationships] dwells." This waiting shapes how we do theology.

Conclusion

Theological thinking is contextual thinking. We are located in a specific social setting and at a particular time in human history. We live outside of Eden. In biblical terms, we are in the groaning creation during the present evil age—indeed the last days.

---

29. D. Broughton Knox, *The Everlasting God: A Character Study of God in the Old and New Testaments* (Hertfordshire, UK: Evangelical Press, 1982), 52.

30. Bob Morrison, Patti Ryan, and Wanda Mallette, "Lookin' for Love," © Sony/ATV Music Publishing LLC, 1980.

It is the world of human brokenness, which bears the marks of the fall and the great rupture. Evil is at work in the world. Indeed, there is a supernatural opponent of God, his word, and his people who is to be taken seriously and not dismissively, lest we embrace the flaw of the excluded middle. In this setting, we live between the cross and the coming again of Jesus.

As a consequence, we are doing theology as pilgrims, as Michael Horton has so usefully reminded us.[31] Living in between means that we are not yet glorified beings, and so we still can make many mistakes as teachers (James 3:2). In that light, humility is a key virtue. Hence, as noted, there is wisdom in the idea of *semper reformanda*, or always reforming in the light of the word of revelation. Teachers of the people of God need themselves to be teachable.

---

31. Michael Horton, *The Christian Faith: A Systematic Theology for Pilgrims on the Way* (Grand Rapids, MI: Zondervan, 2011).

4

The Work of Wisdom

The question now arises as to how the three elements above should be related to each other: the word of revelation, the witness of Christian thought, and the world of human brokenness. This, I believe, is a work of wisdom.

But what is wisdom? In biblical perspective, wisdom is not reducible to the accumulation of data, information gathering, or knowledge acquisition, even though all three have their place. Wisdom knows what to do with data, information, and knowledge for both thought and life. Moreover, wisdom is predicated on an attitude: the fear of the Lord.

The fear of the LORD is the beginning of knowledge;
  fools despise wisdom and instruction. (Prov. 1:7)

This reverent attitude recognizes that God is God and that we are not God. The contrast is striking between the wise person characterized by one attitude and the fool by another. Additionally, wisdom involves an activity of both acute and astute observation. The wise person knows how to pay attention to reality and take instruction from what is seen. Proverbs 6:6–11 provides a good example:

Go to the ant, O sluggard;
> consider her ways, and be wise.
Without having any chief,
> officer, or ruler,
she prepares her bread in summer
> and gathers her food in harvest.

The lesson is then drawn:

How long will you lie there, O sluggard?
> When will you arise from your sleep?
A little sleep, a little slumber,
> a little folding of the hands to rest,
and poverty will come upon you like a robber,
> and want like an armed man.

The wise person prospers, the fool does not. The wise person can make a connection between what is observed in nature (the ant's behavior in summer with winter coming) and human life.

In theology, wisdom is reasoning employed as the servant of Scripture and not as the master of Scripture. I have chosen "reasoning" quite deliberately. Reason must not be reified as though it were a thing separate from us. Reason does not function on its own, in a spiritual vacuum. *Persons* reason. *Persons* mount arguments, question or demolish them, and marshal or dismiss evidence. And persons do that either in submission to God or in conflict with him.

So where does human reasoning fit in the story of wisdom? It was the philosopher William James (1842–1910) who defined philosophy as "the unusually stubborn attempt to think clearly."[1] No less a stubborn attempt is necessary for doing

---

1. Quoted in Gary E. Kessler, *Voices of Wisdom: A Multicultural Philosophy Reader* (Belmont, CA: Wadsworth, 1992), 9. Wisdom is especially needed when we appeal to Scripture to address issues not mentioned in Scripture (e.g., abortion). It is important to make a distinction between philosophy as an activity of careful thought and philosophy

theology or reasoning in general. Yet reason can only ever be *norma normata* (a ruled norm), as we've seen. To place reason above Scripture was the error of the Sadducees. Jesus chided them, "You are wrong, because you know neither the Scriptures nor the power of God" (Matt. 22:29). Their formal mistake lay in their ignorance of relevant Scripture. Their material mistake was their not seeing how Exodus 3:6 affected the resurrection question.

Importantly, there is a moral dimension to knowing. Early in the twentieth century, the Scottish theologian P. T. Forsyth captured that dimension in writing: "Logic is rooted in Ethic, for the truth we see depends upon the men we are."[2] Forsyth must not be misunderstood. He did not argue that the truth depends upon the kind of moral agents we are. But our ability to recognize the truth, see the truth, has a moral component. Virtue epistemology has its place.[3] Jesus taught that it is the pure in heart who see God (Matt. 5:8). It is those who do the will of God who know (John 7:17). In fact, the wise person is the virtuous one.

Some may think that the fall has so damaged the human mind that without the aid of the Spirit there can be no true thought about anything. Some confuse this notion with the noetic effects of sin.[4] However, Jesus thought that the crowds were able to interpret natural phenomena like weather patterns (e.g.,

---

as the doctrines taught by this philosopher or that, which may be thoroughly anti-Christian (see, e.g., Daniel C. Dennett, *Breaking the Spell: Religion as a Natural Phenomenon*). The theologian can greatly profit from knowing and using the tools generated by the activity of philosophy (e.g., conceptual analysis). Christians who are philosophers and theologians who can philosophize have their place in the theological enterprise.

2. P. T. Forsyth, *The Principle of Authority in Relation to Certainty, Sanctity and Society: An Essay in the Philosophy of Experimental Religion*, 2nd ed. (London: Independent Press, 1952), 9.

3. Indeed, the wise person is characterized by virtue, and the foolish one is characterized by vice. It is also important to recognize that the possession of knowledge does not guarantee either virtue or wisdom. Paul wrote to the Corinthians how knowledge can puff one up (1 Cor. 8:1).

4. *Nous* is the Greek word for "mind."

Luke 12:54–56). Moreover, he expected Nicodemus as a teacher of Israel to have understood his teaching about the new birth, even though Nicodemus needed the new birth himself (John 3:1–10). Nicodemus asked, "How can these things be?" (v. 9). Jesus's reply had a certain sharpness to it: "Are you the teacher of Israel and yet you do not understand these things?" (v. 10). Even Pilate understood on some level what Jesus was claiming, though he did not believe it: "Pilate also wrote an inscription and put it on the cross. It read, 'Jesus of Nazareth, the King of the Jews'" (John 19:19). The chief priests also understood what Jesus was claiming but wanted the inscription nuanced: "Many of the Jews read this inscription, for the place where Jesus was crucified was near the city, and it was written in Aramaic, in Latin, and in Greek. So the chief priests of the Jews said to Pilate, 'Do not write, "The King of the Jews," but rather, "This man said, I am King of the Jews"'" (John 19:20–21).

Sin causes not a cognitive disability but an affective disinclination to trust in God, honor him, or give thanks to him (Rom. 1:21). As both John Calvin and Jonathan Edwards taught, the Spirit in the new birth changes our affections so that we embrace the things of God.[5] In particular, this change in our affections shows itself in our hospitable reception to the word of God (see Acts 17:17; 1 Thess. 2:13; and in contrast, 1 Cor. 2:13–14).[6] There is, therefore, a crucial spiritual dimension to knowing God through his word.

---

5. I have on my bookshelf a New Testament study Bible annotated by Jewish scholars. I was struck, in reading the notes on, e.g., Eph. 2:8–10, that I could have written them myself. The writer understands what Paul is asserting about salvation by faith and not works. But believing it is another thing. See Amy-Jill Levine and Marc Zvi Brettler, eds., *The Jewish Annotated New Testament* (New York: Oxford University Press, 2011), 347.

6. Was a change in affection also the experience of Old Testament saints? This question raises the issue of whether Old Testament believers were born again, and with it the matter of the continuity or discontinuity between the old covenant and the new covenant. On this question see Graham A. Cole, *He Who Gives Life: The Doctrine of the Holy Spirit* (Wheaton, IL: Crossway, 2007), 143–45. I argue that indeed Old Testament believers were regenerated.

The Appeal to Reason in Scripture

In so many of the prophetic writings of the Old Testament, God is arguing his case against his people, who have trodden under foot their covenant with him. Even so, God comes with an invitation:

> Come now, let us reason together, says the LORD:
> though your sins are like scarlet,
>   they shall be as white as snow,
> though they are red like crimson,
>   they shall become like wool. (Isa. 1:18)

The sins in view are delineated in the earlier part of Isaiah 1: rebellion, iniquity, corruption, vain offerings, and blood on guilty hands. The prospect of a change of fortune is offered:

> If you are willing and obedient,
>   you shall eat the good of the land. (v. 19)

Then logic of the alternative is spelled out:

> But if you refuse and rebel,
>   you shall be eaten by the sword;
>   for the mouth of the LORD has spoken. (v. 20)

In Isaiah 41, God challenges the gods of the nations:

> Set forth your case, says the LORD;
>   bring your proofs, says the King of Jacob. (v. 21)

Among other things, the God of Israel can declare what is to come (vv. 22–23). The gods are impotent on that point (v. 24). As in a courtroom, the living God knows how to argue and mount a case.

In the New Testament we see Jesus in debate with opponents and using well-known forms of logical argument. Indeed, philosopher Dallas Willard describes Jesus as "the Logician" because of "his use of logic and his obvious powers of logical thinking as manifested in the Gospels of the New Testament."[7] Mark 3 presents an interesting example. Jesus's ministry in Galilee has attracted scribes from Jerusalem to come down and take a look. They cannot deny the miraculous. Instead, they offer an alternative explanation: Jesus's exorcisms are the work of the devil, not God. Jesus counters:

> And he called them to him and said to them in parables, "How can Satan cast out Satan? If a kingdom is divided against itself, that kingdom cannot stand. And if a house is divided against itself, that house will not be able to stand. And if Satan has risen up against himself and is divided, he cannot stand, but is coming to an end." (vv. 23–26)

This example is a classic *reductio ad absurdum* (reduction to absurdity) argument. If the scribes were right, then think it through: Satan would be in the process of self-destruction by destroying his own minions. Jesus offers a much more plausible explanation with his own self-reference implied: "But no one can enter a strong man's house and plunder his goods, unless he first binds the strong man. Then indeed he may plunder his house" (v. 27).

Jesus also uses argument in a positive way to instruct disciples. So, to encourage prayer, for example, he teaches in the Sermon on the Mount, "If you then, who are evil, know how to give good gifts to your children, how much more will your Father who is in heaven give good things to those who ask him!"

7. Dallas Willard, "Jesus the Logician," Dallas Willard (website), http://www.dwillard .org/articles/artview.asp?artID=39, accessed November 29, 2017. Also see Juan Valdes, "Jesus: The Master of Critical Thinking," Reasons for Hope (website), https://www.rforh .com/resources/know-it/diving-deeper/jesus-the-master-of-critical-thinking, accessed November 29, 2017.

(Matt. 7:11). This is an *a fortiori* (for the stronger) argument. If the lesser is so, how much more the greater.[8]

The apostle Paul also knew how to appeal to reason. He offers the Corinthians a cumulative case for believing in Christ's resurrection. The Old Testament Scriptures predicted resurrection. The risen Christ was seen by the apostles, his brother James, by Paul himself, and some five hundred others, most of whom were still alive at the time of Paul's writing (1 Cor. 15:1–11). But Paul does not leave it at that. He also explores the logic of the alternative in a series of hypothetical syllogisms (1 Cor. 15:12–19). If Christ were not risen, then what would follow step after step? The logical form of this part of his case is called a *sorites*.

Peter in his first letter makes the point more generally when he calls for "always being prepared to make a defense [*apologia*, "apology"] to anyone who asks you for a reason for the hope [the gospel] that is in you." Christians are to share not only what they believe but also why they believe it when challenged to do so. Defending the faith is Christian apology, and such a defense requires a reason (*logos*, "word," "reason").

In the light of the cumulative testimony of both the Old Testament and the New, the appeal to reasoning has its place in the life of God's people. Biblical religion is a religion of the heart, but in biblical thought the heart includes the mind.[9]

Some Tools for Wise Theological Thinking

To do certain jobs, our hands need the right tools. I had to fix a wobbly chair the other day and I needed a Phillips-head

---

8. The book of Hebrews offers an a fortiori argument in Heb. 9:13–14: "For if the blood of goats and bulls, and the sprinkling of defiled persons with the ashes of a heifer, sanctify for the purification of the flesh, how much more [a fortiori] will the blood of Christ, who through the eternal Spirit offered himself without blemish to God, purify our conscience from dead works to serve the living God."

9. For an excellent discussion of reason in the service of God, see John Webster, *Holiness* (Grand Rapids, MI: Eerdmans, 2003), 10–30. I am grateful to Oren Martin for reminding me of this fine work.

screwdriver to do so. The mind also needs tools to enable wise thought. The wise person knows the importance of categories and distinctions as tools for clear thought. Here are some that I have found helpful in thinking, speaking, and writing theologically.

Dogmatic Rank

Dogmatic rank is fundamental to wise theological thinking. The phrase means that teachings need to be ranked, and the ranking has to do with importance for faithfulness and fellowship. Not all teachings we hold have the same importance, although all biblical teaching is important.

Jesus shows us the category in action. In Matthew 23 we see him announce to his disciples and the crowds a series of woes against the scribes and Pharisees. Among them is this one: "Woe to you, scribes and Pharisees, hypocrites! For you tithe mint and dill and cumin, and have neglected the weightier matters of the law: justice and mercy and faithfulness. These you ought to have done, without neglecting the others" (v. 23). Scrupulosity had triumphed over deeper values. There are weightier matters of the Torah. However, it is not either–or but a matter of rank.

The notion of dogmatic rank I tease out along these lines. I distinguish between level 1 convictions, level 2 convictions, opinions, and speculations. An example of a level 1 conviction is that salvation is, as Galatians teaches, by grace alone—not by grace and works or by works alone. The doctrine of justification by grace through faith alone is the gospel recovered by the Reformers of the sixteenth century. Another level 1 conviction is that Christ is truly God as well as truly human, which 1 John 4 teaches. It is hard to see how one can have Christian fellowship with someone who denies this biblical truth. These are convictions vital to the gospel and warranted by Scripture.

However, when the question is whether an infant may be baptized (paedobaptism) or only those who profess faith for themselves are to be baptized (credobaptism), I argue that this is a level 2 conviction. One can have real Christian fellowship with someone who holds a different view on this matter.[10] Level 2 convictions are particularly relevant when identifying churches and denominations.

An opinion is a thought-out theological position, but it should not affect the circle of Christian fellowship. I may hold that the gifts of the Holy Spirit mentioned in Acts and 1 Corinthians have continued or ceased and argue strongly for my view without de-churching the person who disagrees with me. As for speculations, not much hangs theologically on whether I speculate that the identity of the antichrist is X or Y.[11]

A useful question to ask in assessing dogmatic rank is, What is lost if a particular conviction is removed from our beliefs?[12] For example, what would be lost if one rejects the practice of making the sign of the cross on the candidate's forehead at baptism? The fact is that many Bible-believing traditions don't make the sign of the cross, although my own does. For a second example, what would be lost if we remove the belief that Jesus Christ is fully God, the Son who became incarnate? In the former case, I would argue that what would be lost would be of small dogmatic weight. However, in the latter case, we lose the doctrines of the Trinity, Christology, and salvation. This

---

10. I am dean at Trinity Evangelical Divinity School, and some faculty are paedobaptists and others are credobaptists without fellowship being threatened.

11. Stanley J. Grenz and Roger E. Olson, *Who Needs Theology? An Invitation to the Study of God* (Downers Grove, IL: InterVarsity Press, 1996), 73–77, offer their own version of this typology. They write of dogma (my level 1), doctrine (my level 2), and opinion. A threefold typology, however termed, is at least as old as the Reformation. See Richard A. Muller, *Latin and Greek Theological Terms: Drawn Principally from Protestant Scholastic Theology* (Grand Rapids, MI: Baker Academic, 2017), 40–41: *articuli fundamentales*, *articuli fundamentales secundarii*, and *articuli non-fundamentales*.

12. Another useful question is to ask whether I can preach what's in view or merely discuss it.

would dissolve Christianity as I know it. Hence, the dogmatic weight is immense.

The classic saying of the Lutheran theologian Rupertus Meldenius (1582–1651) is appropriate here. He lived through the Thirty Years' War (1618–1648) between Catholics and Protestants. In a tract on Christian unity published around 1627, he argued, "In the essential, unity, and in the non-essentials, liberty, and in all things, charity."[13]

Reason and Imagination

The living God of the Bible is unimaginable—that is to say, beyond visualizing. Hence, there are the pervasive biblical ban on the making of images and diatribes against the folly of idol making. The Ten Commandments are clear: "You shall not make for yourself a carved image, or any likeness of anything that is in heaven above, or that is in the earth beneath, or that is in the water under the earth" (Ex. 20:4). The New Testament echoes the Old Testament in 1 John 5:21: "Little children, keep yourselves from idols." Paul sees idol making as an expression of human folly in Romans 1:22–23: "Claiming to be wise, they became fools, and exchanged the glory of the immortal God for images resembling mortal man and birds and animals and creeping things." Both Isaiah and Jeremiah satirize idol making (e.g., Isa. 44:6–20; Jer. 10:1–5). However, what God has revealed about himself and his plans is conceivable. That is to say, one can form a logically coherent thought with revelatory concepts.

The concept of the Trinity is a case in point.[14] To claim that there are three persons in one person or three Gods in one God

---

13. Mark Ross, "In the Essentials Unity, In Non-Essentials Liberty, In All Things Charity," Ligonier Ministries (website), https://www.ligonier.org/learn/articles/essentials-unity-non-essentials-liberty-all-things/, accessed December 15, 2017.

14. The term "Trinity" is not in the Bible. The key question, though, is not whether the word is in the text but whether the idea or concept of Trinity is there. As B. B. Warfield argued concerning the doctrine of the Trinity, in some cases an extrabiblical term

is, at best, confusing and, at worst, contradictory. However, to claim that there is one God in three persons is not contradictory, even though it is mysterious. Importantly, the concept of the Trinity is unimaginable. I cannot form anything like an adequate mental picture of the Trinity. Three bearded male-like figures in discussion on a cloud simply won't do.

Many of this world's applicable concepts are likewise conceivable but not imaginable. I cannot picture in my mind a subatomic particle like a quark, but I have good reasons for believing such exists, although unseen. The distinction between the unimaginable and the conceivable is important because I suspect that there are Christians who deep down wonder if, in being asked to worship the Trinity, they are being asked to believe in nonsense. It is so easy to think that only the imaginable is conceivable.

Other Christian doctrines are likewise conceivable but unimaginable—that is to say, beyond mental imaging. For example, I cannot imagine how Jesus is one person who is both truly God and truly human, but I can tell the story of the incarnation without falling into incoherence.[15]

Reason, Faith, Fear, and Sight

Traditionally in the philosophy of religion there is discussion of the relation of faith and reason. One could be forgiven for thinking that there is a thing called reason and a thing called faith apart from persons (the reification problem I mentioned earlier, p. 70). The fact is that persons reason and persons

captures the sense of Scripture when simply quoting Scripture does not. After all, the devil knew how to quote Scripture, and so did Arius in the fourth century. See B. B. Warfield, *Biblical Foundations* (London: Tyndale Press, 1958), 70–110.

15. A good example of how Christian philosophy can aid the work of theology can be found in Thomas V. Morris, *The Logic of God Incarnate* (Eugene, OR: Wipf and Stock, 2001). Morris, as an analytical philosopher using philosophical tools, examines carefully and defends strongly the coherence of claiming that Jesus is truly God and truly human.

believe. Reasoning does not happen apart from persons; neither does faith. Persons also fear. Persons also see. How reason, faith, fear, and sight relate needs wise treatment. We saw earlier in this chapter that Scripture contains numerous examples of reasoning. The reality is that in Scripture the great contrast is not between trusting and reasoning but between trusting and fearing, and between trusting and seeing.

Jesus and Paul help us see the contrast. In a famous incident in the Gospels, the disciples are in a boat with Jesus when a storm hits. Jesus is asleep. They panic. We read in Mark 4:38–40, "And they woke him and said to him, 'Teacher, do you not care that we are perishing?' And he awoke and rebuked the wind and said to the sea, 'Peace! Be still!' And the wind ceased, and there was a great calm. He said to them, 'Why are you so afraid? Have you still no faith?'" Faith is only as good as its object. Jesus can be trusted to protect them from the storm. Paul, in 2 Corinthians 5:6–7, writes about the world to come in these terms: "So we are always of good courage. We know that while we are at home in the body we are away from the Lord, for we walk by faith, not by sight." The writer to the Hebrews adds to our picture: "Now faith is the assurance of things hoped for, the conviction of things not seen" (11:1). It is a perennial temptation to turn faith into sight.[16] Hence, the temptation is to make idols as Israel did in Moses's day at Sinai (Ex. 32:1–8).

Control Beliefs

Philosopher Nicholas Wolterstorff has developed a theory of theories. The details of it need not detain us. One element is particularly important to doing theology wisely. Wolterstorff argues that when we theorize about anything, control beliefs

---

16. In technical terms, to attempt to turn faith into sight is "overrealized eschatology," as though the world to come can be experienced now in all its fullness. Such a view of the future undermines the Christian hope (cf. Rom. 24–25; 1 John 3:1–2).

operate. A control belief acts as a gatekeeper to what we admit as a candidate for knowledge or not.[17] For example, if a theological claim contradicts the word of revelation, then I will reject it. The Jehovah's Witnesses reduce the Holy Spirit to a mere impersonal force, which makes no sense of the Spirit's praying for us, described in Romans 8:26. A vitally important task in doing theology is to find the key control beliefs for faithful doctrines of God, Christ, the Holy Spirit, the church, and so on. Indeed, in a later chapter I will use this idea of control beliefs to help construct a doctrine of the Trinity.

The Discipline of Biblical Theology

Wise theological thinking uses the word of revelation in the most faithful and responsible way. In my view, that means employing biblical theology in the construction of doctrine. By biblical theology, I mean that disciplined way of reading Scripture canonically that places any text in its context, both its immediate literary unit and its place in the canon in the light of redemptive history's unfolding, from Genesis 1 to Revelation 22.[18]

There will always be a place for the proof text in doing theology.[19] Why do I believe in the incarnation? I do so because of John 1:14. A proof text can save time. However, what do I do if someone goes on to ask me the reason I have cited that particular text. In that case, I need to put John 1:14 in the context of John 1:1–18, which is the prologue to the Gospel of John.

---

17. Nicholas Wolterstorff, *Reason within the Bounds of Reason*, 2nd ed. (Grand Rapids, MI: Eerdmans, 1984), 69–70.

18. For an excellent treatment of the flow of redemptive history and its import for doing theology, see Richard Lints, *The Fabric of Theology: A Prolegomena to Evangelical Theology* (Grand Rapids, MI: Eerdmans, 1993), 293–310, especially his idea of the "three horizons" of interpretation. I am grateful to Oren Martin for drawing my attention to this work.

19. For an able and nuanced defense of proof-texting, see R. Michael Allen and Scott R. Swain, "In Defense of Proof-Texting," The Evangelical Theological Society (website), http://www.etsjets.org/files/JETS-PDFs/54/54-3/JETS_54-3_589–606_Allen%20&%20Swain.pdf, accessed July 23, 2018. I am grateful to Oren Martin for bringing this article to my notice.

I need to know that it is new covenant literature, and in terms of the canon it presupposes the old covenant. So, in terms of redemptive history, it is found in these last days in which God has spoken to us by his Son (Heb. 1:1–2).

Using a biblical theology approach such as this safeguards us from citing texts out of context when addressing the normative questions of what we ought to believe, what we should value, and how we ought to live. The worst case of citing a text out of context in my experience was to hear a student preach on the text "I go to prepare a place for you" from John 14:2 and then proceed to give a sermon on hell. Such a misuse of Scripture was heartbreaking. He had neglected the key steps in doing biblical theology. He was trying to connect the text to the present, but he did so in a way that ignored the immediate context of the text in John, let alone its wider context in John and its place in the canon of Scripture.

Three Important Criteria

A criterion provides a standard by which something may be judged. In the United States, being thirty-five years of age or older is a criterion for eligibility to run for president. Wise thinking in doing theology has standards too. There are three that I have found particularly helpful.

The first criterion is the scriptural one. Does a theological claim or proposal have scriptural warrant? Is it consistent with what we find in the Scriptures? "Where stands it written?" is a fair question. The second is the rational criterion. Are we being asked to believe in nonsense or the self-contradictory? I cannot believe in square circles because, on analysis, if you understand the two terms, it is an incoherent conjunction of ideas. Lastly, livability is a criterion. Am I able to live as though my claim or theological proposal were true? Can my operational theology match my espoused one? I may claim to be sinlessly perfect, but do my words and deeds undermine such a claim? What about the pride that such a view might express?

The Power of the Question

History knows several masters of the question. In Western thought, Socrates (d. 399 BC) is often considered the quintessential question asker. He famously compared himself to a stinging fly who, through his questioning, sought to stir sleepy Athenian citizens into life. In his apology—given before his fellow Athenian citizens in the context of the trial for his life— he said colorfully, "The state is like a big thoroughbred horse, so big that he is a bit slow and heavy, and wants a gadfly to wake him up."[20]

The unexamined life is not worth living, he argued. An examined life is a questioning life. Socrates was clear in his method. In reply to his accusers, he argued, "If again I say it is the greatest good for a man every day to discuss virtue and the other things about which you hear me talking and examining myself and everybody else, and that life without enquiry is not worth living for a man, you will believe me still less if I say that."[21] What is piety? What is justice? What is beauty? These and other questions he asked, and ultimately it cost him his life. He became the great philosophical martyr as a result.

An even greater than Socrates is Jesus. He too knew the power of the right question. Think about his well-known parable of the Good Samaritan in Luke 10. Jesus closed with the question of who was a neighbor to the poor, beaten-up Jew on the road to Jericho: "Which of these three [the priest, the Levite, and the Samaritan], do you think, proved to be a neighbor

20. Socrates, "The Apology," in *Great Dialogues of Plato*, ed. Eric H. Warmington and Philip G. Rouse, trans. W. H. D. Rouse (New York: Mentor, 1956), 436.

21. Socrates, "The Apology," 443.

to the man who fell among the robbers?" (v. 36). Jesus asked searching, disturbing questions right up to his crucifixion. His exchange with Pharisees in the temple in the week before his death is instructive:

> Now while the Pharisees were gathered together, Jesus asked them a question, saying, "What do you think about the Christ? Whose son is he?" They said to him, "The son of David." He said to them, "How is it then that David, in the Spirit, calls him Lord, saying,
>
>> "'The Lord said to my Lord,
>> "Sit at my right hand,
>>> until I put your enemies under your feet"'?
>
> If then David calls him Lord, how is he his son?" (Matt. 22:41–45)

The response of those who heard him shows just how searching Jesus's question was: "And no one was able to answer him a word, nor from that day did anyone dare to ask him any more questions" (Matt. 22:46).

To do theology wisely outside of Eden we need to be informed by at least four categories of questions. First, there is the factual question. In the first instance we ask whether there is biblical testimony relevant to addressing the issue at hand. If the issue is whether human evildoing is a matter of sin or a lack of education, what does the Bible say? Another factual question would be whether any great Christian thinker past or present has considered the problem in view. For example, Augustine had much to say about human sin, as did John Calvin.

A second important question is the semantic or conceptual one. What is meant by the words used to articulate a particular problem? For example, what do we mean by the word "sin"?

What do we mean by "education"? A third question is the moral one. What ought we to answer? This question has great relevance if the answer rightly attracts either praise or blame. For example, is obtaining an abortion always sin? The last question is the pastoral one. How will my answer affect relationships? For example, the person asking the abortion question may have had one.

Conclusion

Doing theology is an exercise in wisdom. Wisdom knows the value of what is seen and heard. Wisdom knows how to make connections that aren't foolish. Wisdom is an activity, but more than that, it is an activity informed by a right attitude of reverence toward God. In particular, wisdom knows how to connect the word of revelation, the witness of Christian thought and practice, and the world of human brokenness. The wise person knows that Scripture is the final court of appeal in any matter of conflict involving putative authorities.

Foolish ways to do theology abound outside of Eden. Tradition may trump revelation from God (e.g., a celibate priesthood). Experience of the broken world may trump revelation from God (e.g., on homosexuality). The claims of autonomous reason may trump the revelation from God (e.g., relativism). However, John Webster admirably reminds us, "As the exercise of holy reason, Christian theology is a *venture undertaken in prayerful dependence upon the Holy Spirit*."[22] May the Spirit of God overrule and direct our steps in the doing of theology.

---

22. Webster, *Holiness*, 22; original emphasis.

5

The Way of Worship

Putting It All Together in Thought and Life

In this chapter, the fifth element, the way of worship, is added to the elements already discussed—the word of revelation, the witness of Christian thought and practice, the world of human brokenness, and the work of wisdom. Here we will explore the doctrine of the Trinity in the light of the normative scriptural testimony and the witness of past and present great Christian thinkers, with an eye on the broken creation of which we are a part. All this is to be done as wisely as possible and as an offering to the living God. It is an exercise in faithful thought.

Faithful thinking ought not to be divorced from faithful living. We are not mere brains on sticks. We are relational beings. Again, faithful thought must not be decoupled from a faithful life. As Grenz and Olson rightly argue, "Good theology is never content to remain on the theoretical level; it always affects life."[1]

---

1. Stanley J. Grenz and Roger E. Olson, *Who Needs Theology? An Invitation to the Study of God* (Downers Grove, IL: InterVarsity Press, 1996), 120.

As I suggested in an earlier chapter, a wise distinction may be made between an espoused theology and an operational one, but not a separation. If our operational theology is to comport with our espoused theology, then we need to embrace the godly disciplines.[2] In fact, a godly life and insight into the things of God are connected. Jesus made this point clear in the Sermon the Mount: "Blessed are the pure in heart, for they shall see God" (Matt. 5:8). He makes a similar claim in John 7:17: "If anyone's will is to do God's will, he will know whether the teaching is from God or whether I am speaking on my own authority." There is relation between virtue and insight. This is the truth in virtue epistemology: the connection between character and insight.

Once more, the doctrine of the Trinity provides a case in point, as can be seen in relation to one of the godly disciplines—namely, prayer. We find wisdom from the early church—the witness of Christian thought and practice—to draw on. As we saw in an earlier chapter, Evagrius Ponticus said: "If you are a theologian, you will pray truly. And if you pray truly, you are a theologian."[3] Present-day theologian Kelly M. Kapic adds his voice: "There can be no substitute for prayer."[4] Indeed, ought not our praying reflect who God is? The New Testament accents our praying to the Father in the name of the Son by the Spirit. This is Trinitarian praying and embodies the gospel of the mediatorship of Christ. Sadly, however, much praying in churches today could be Unitarian: "Dear God . . . Amen!" No wonder some confuse the Allah of Islam with the God of Christian Scripture.

---

2. For very helpful discussions of the godly disciplines, see R. Kent Hughes, *Disciplines of a Godly Man* (Wheaton, IL: Crossway, 2001), and Barbara Hughes, *Disciplines of a Godly Woman* (Wheaton, IL: Crossway, 2006).

3. Evagrius Ponticus, "On Prayer," par. 61, The Desert Fathers (blog), http://desert fathers.blogspot.com/2011/06/works-of-evagrius-ponticuson-prayer.html, accessed April 28, 2016.

4. Kelly M. Kapic, *A Little Book for New Theologians: Why and How to Study Theology* (Downers Grove, IL: IVP Academic, 2012), 66.

In this chapter I attempt to show what theologizing looks like in practice. The topic is the nature of God as Trinity. Let's see how the word of revelation, the witness of Christian thought and practice, and the world of human brokenness may be related by the work of wisdom to our expression of worship. We start by visiting an instructive debate from the past.

The Chalcedonian Way

In an earlier chapter we examined the value of the witness of Christian thought and practice. How those before us went about the task of theologizing for the sake of the church exhibits a wisdom worth retrieving. The Chalcedonian Definition of AD 451 serves as a case in point.[5] Some 318 church leaders gathered at Chalcedon to address a particular wrong view of Jesus known to history as Eutycheanism.[6] The details of the synod need not detain us, but what these fathers did is worth noting. They articulated the following doctrine of Christ:

> Following the holy Fathers we teach with one voice that the Son [of God] and our Lord Jesus Christ is to be confessed as one and the same [Person], that he is perfect in Godhead and perfect in manhood, very God and very man, of a reasonable soul and [human] body consisting, consubstantial with the Father as touching his Godhead, and consubstantial with us as touching his manhood; made in all things like unto us, sin only excepted; begotten of his Father before the worlds according to his Godhead; but in

---

5. Chalcedon was in what is now modern Turkey. Interestingly, the seven ecumenical creeds, of which Chalcedon is one, were promulgated not in Europe but in Asia Minor, and not in what is now the West.

6. Eutyches (AD 378–456) was the head of a large monastery outside Constantinople. He argued that in the incarnation the divine and human were mingled to constitute one nature, like a drop of honey mingled with the ocean. See the discussion by H. D. McDonald, "Monophysitism," in *New Dictionary of Theology Historical and Systematic*, 2nd ed., ed. Martin Davie, Tim Glass, Stephen R. Holmes, John McDowell, and T. A Noble (Downers Grove, IL: InterVarsity Press, 2016), 591.

these last days for us men and for our salvation born [into
the world] of the Virgin Mary, the Mother of God according to his manhood.[7]

Key Christological control beliefs concerning the incarnation are in evidence:

- Jesus Christ is one person.
- He has two natures.
- He is truly God.
- He is truly human.

These claims constitute the Christian's firewall against wrong
views of Jesus.[8] If we deny that Jesus is one person, we are into
Nestorianism.[9] If, on the one hand, we deny that he is God, we
have a low Christology (doctrine of Christ) that reduces Jesus
to a mere human prophet or sage. Islam is a case in point. Jesus
in Islamic thought is the second-greatest human prophet, next
to Muhammad. If, on the other hand, we deny his humanity, we
have a spirit only appearing as human, as in versions of ancient
Gnosticism.[10]

Importantly, these early Christians made no attempt to explain the *how* of incarnation. No metaphysical explanation is
in view. Instead, boundaries are set. That is what I term "the
Chalcedonian way." To deny that Christ is one person is to
cross the boundary. So too is the denial that he has two natures
and is truly God and truly human. At the very least our theolo-

---

7. For the full statement, see "Chalcedonian Definition of Faith," Early Church
Texts (website), http://www.earlychurchtexts.com/public/chalcedonian_definition.htm,
accessed August 29, 2017.

8. A heresy is a wrong doctrinal position that is toxic to the health of the church.

9. Recall the reference to Nestorianism in the introduction, p. 15.

10. "Gnosticism" is an umbrella term that, historically speaking, applied to a number
of second-century sects which prized knowledge (Greek, *gnōsis*, "knowledge") from
and about the spirit world. Salvation came through such knowledge and enlightenment.
These sects were elitist and escapist, arguing for the need to flee from the material world.
There appear to have been anticipations of these views even within the New Testament
era (e.g., 1 John 4:1–6).

gizing should find and define the relevant boundaries on every theological topic. There is room for opinion and speculation as to the *how* of incarnation. But opinion and speculation need to observe the boundaries, if those boundaries can be shown to be warranted by the word of revelation.[11]

How then are the boundaries to be drawn?

Boundary Drawing and the Appeal to Scripture

The well-known evangelical theologian Millard J. Erickson offers a helpful analysis of how Scripture is to be used in constructing doctrine. He writes:

> Our theology will consist of various types of theological statements that can be classified on the basis of their derivation. It is important to attribute to each type of statement an appropriate degree of authority.
>
> 1. Direct statements of Scripture are to be accorded the greatest weight. To the degree that they accurately represent what the Bible teaches, they have the status of a direct word from God. Great care must of course be exercised to make certain that we are dealing here with the teaching of Scripture, and not an interpretation imposed upon it.[12]
>
> 2. Direct implications of Scripture must also be given high priority. They are to be regarded as slightly less authoritative than direct statements, however, because the introduction of an additional step (logical inference) carries with it the possibility of interpretational error.[13]

---

11. As mentioned earlier, a good example of metaphysical faith seeking understanding can be found in Thomas V. Morris, *The Logic of God Incarnate* (Eugene, OR: Wipf and Stock, 2001).

12. These examples come to mind: Jesus Christ is one person (Eph. 4:4–6); he is truly God (John 1:14), and he is truly human (John 1:14).

13. This example comes to mind: Christ has two natures: truly God and truly human. Scripture does not state in any direct way that Christ has two natures. The claim is a direct implication.

3. Probable implications of Scripture, that is, inferences that are drawn in cases where one of the assumptions or premises is only probable, are somewhat less authoritative than direct implications. While deserving respect, such statements should be held with a certain amount of tentativeness.[14]

4. Inductive conclusions from Scripture vary in their degree of authority. Inductive investigation, of course, gives only probabilities. The certainty of its conclusions increases as the proportion between the number of references actually considered and the total number of pertinent references that could conceivably be considered increases.[15]

5. Conclusions inferred from the general revelation, which is less particularized and less explicit than the special revelation, must, accordingly, always be subject to the clearer and more explicit statements of the Bible.[16]

6. Outright speculations, which frequently include hypotheses based on a single statement or hint in Scripture, or derived from somewhat obscure or unclear parts of the Bible, may also be stated and utilized by the theologians. There is no harm in this, as long as the theologian is aware and warns the reader or hearer of what is being done. A serious problem enters if these speculations are presented with the same degree of authoritativeness attributed to statements of the first category listed above.[17]

The theologian will want to employ all of the legitimate material available, giving it in each case neither more

---

14. Unfortunately, Erickson gives no examples of any of his categories. With regard to this one, I am somewhat at a loss to provide one.

15. Some claim that Jesus did his mighty messianic works in the power of his Holy Spirit–anointed humanity and not his deity. This claim is based on a synthesis of numerous biblical texts and in my view is highly probable (e.g., Acts 10:34–38).

16. Again, unfortunately, Erickson gives no examples of any of his categories. I am somewhat at a loss to provide one here.

17. For example, some elaborate Christologies have been built on the one mention that Jesus humbly "emptied himself" in Phil. 2:7 (Greek, *ekenōsen*, "emptied"). Indeed, there is a whole family of kenotic Christologies. That Christ emptied himself is a biblical fact. Explaining that reality in detail is the challenge.

nor less credence than is appropriate in view of the nature of its sources.[18]

There is much wisdom in Erickson's analysis. Technically speaking, Scripture presents a material system and not a formal one. In a formal system, implications strictly follow. For example, if A is greater than B and B is greater than C, then A is greater than C. However, in a material system, implications are trickier to unravel. If John is Mary's husband, then he is male by definition. However, if I claim that he was married after he turned eighteen and had left high school, I may be right, but further evidence is needed. It does not strictly follow. For example, in Illinois, where I live, "with parental consent, a person can marry at sixteen."[19]

The Doctrine of the Trinity

The doctrine of the Trinity is not the product of human research or armchair reasoning about the nature of reality. It is predicated on special revelation with its narrative of the saving work of the one God as Father, Son, and Holy Spirit found in the Scriptures. Based on the testimonies of Scripture the following claims are warranted:

- There is only one God (Deut. 6:4–5; Mark 12:29).
- The Father is God (Matt. 11:25; John 6:27).
- The Son is God (John 1:1; 20:28).
- The Holy Spirit is God (Acts 5:3–4).
- The Father, Son, and Holy Spirit are distinct (John 14–16 passim).
- The Father is personal (Matt. 6:9).
- The Son is personal (Mark 14:62).

---

18. Millard J. Erickson, *Christian Theology*, 3rd ed. (Grand Rapids, MI: Baker Academic, 2013), 65–66.

19. "State-by-State Marriage 'Age of Consent Laws,'" FindLaw (website), http://family.findlaw.com/marriage/state-by-state-marriage-age-of-consent-laws.html, accessed May 3, 2019.

- The Spirit is personal (Rom. 8:26).
- The Father, Son, and Holy Spirit are not separate (Matt. 28:18–20).
- The Father, Son, and Holy Spirit coinhere (John 14–17).

These ten claims constitute the circle of orthodoxy, or right belief.[20] The circle represents what we ought to believe, which is one of our three normative questions.

The Doctrinal Butte

In some ways a doctrinal circle is like a butte. A butte is a landform that is a high hill with a flat top surrounded by steep sides. The sides are taller than the top is wide. Good examples are found in Monument Valley, Navajo Nation, Arizona. There is room on the top to adopt different standing places, but stray too far and you fall off and down the steep sides. In a doctrinal circle I may prefer where I stand to where you stand, but we are in relation to one another on the top of the butte. We share the theological space.

Let us return to the Chalcedonian way for the moment and apply it to our discussion of the Trinity. To deny the oneness of God or the deity of each member of the Godhead or the distinctiveness of the three persons or the personal nature of Father, Son, and Holy Spirit, or the inseparability of the persons or their coinherence (mutual indwelling) is to cross the boundary, move out of the circle of orthodoxy, and fall off the butte.

The Triune God and the World of Human Brokenness

The triune God is a being in communion. Jesus's prayer in John 17 shows us this. He prays to his righteous and holy Father and in doing so refers to the love between them, as well as the glory

---

20. This is a slightly modified version of what D. B. Knox taught me in his doctrine class.

shared by them before there was even a created world (cf. John 17:5, 24–26). This is astounding. Love, communication, and fellowship of persons have always been at the center of reality with or without a created order. The highest blessing of the gospel, as J. I. Packer has shown, is that we are embraced in that communion through our adoption as the children of God. Packer writes:

> Adoption is a *family* idea, conceived in terms of *love*, and viewing God as *father*. In adoption, God takes us into His family and fellowship, and establishes us as His children and heirs. Closeness, affection and generosity are at the heart of the relationship. To be right with God the judge is a great thing, but to be loved and cared for by God the father is greater.[21]

Packer is so right as evidenced by the fact that the very prayer language of Jesus can be our own (e.g., Mark 14:36; Rom. 8:15; Gal. 4:6).

We should not be surprised, then, to see in the world outside Eden a hunger for relationship. How many of our films, TV shows, and plays, as well as songs, are about relationships: found, lost, and recovered? We are created for relationship with our relational God and with one another. This is one of the ways we image God. D. B. Knox captures the point well:

> Through the revelation of the Trinity we learn that the living God, the good and true God, is a God who has relationship within himself, and that the values of relationships ultimately belong to reality in its most absolute form. In the light of this doctrine, personal relationships are seen to be ultimate, are seen to be the most real things that are.[22]

---

21. J. I. Packer, *Knowing God* (London: Hodder and Stoughton, 1973), 185–86; original emphases.

22. Tony Payne, ed., *D. Broughton Knox: Selected Works*, vol. 1, *The Doctrine of God* (Kingsford, NSW: Matthias Media, 2000), 75.

According to Knox, other-person-centeredness characterizes the Trinity and should characterize us as made in the divine image.[23]

The doctrine of the Trinity informs our answers to the two other normative questions at the heart of the theological task: What ought we to value, and how ought we to live? We ought to value the relational and its other-person-centeredness. We ought to live as Paul told us to: "Love one another with brotherly affection. Outdo one another in showing honor" (Rom. 12:10).

A Caveat

This brief work follows the logical order. God has spoken, and so the word of revelation comes first. Next, we see the impact of the revelation unfolding though church history. To do this task we must be aware of our context in the broken world which itself needs redemption. Relating these elements together requires wisdom and is to be offered to God as an expression of our reasonable worship (more on this shortly). However, the order in life may change the order in which we give attention to these things. A circumstance in the broken world may send us back to the word of revelation and then to the witness of Christian thought and practice for further light. For example, encounters with refugees may drive you to Scripture to see how refugees ought to be treated and then how Christians have addressed such a need in past eras. So you need to respond prayerfully. The starting point for theologizing may differ, but Scripture always remains the touchstone of truth.

A Case in Point: Praying to the Holy Spirit

Is it proper to pray to the Holy Spirit? Answering this question seems straightforward, since God is Trinity. J. I. Packer makes

---

23. Payne, *D. Broughton Knox*, 75–76.

the case: "There is no example of doing this anywhere in Scripture, but since the Spirit is God it cannot be wrong to invoke and address him if there is good reason to do so."[24] Packer is right; the Trinity is three persons in one God, and any of the persons may be addressed in prayer. In fact, there are examples of prayer addressed to the Son in the New Testament (e.g., Acts 7:59–60; 1 Cor. 1:2; Heb. 4:14–16). However, Jesus taught us to pray to "our Father in heaven" (Matt. 6:9), and we see this practice in the Pauline Epistles (e.g., Eph. 3:14–21).

Theologically considered, the genius of praying to the Father in the name of Son in reliance upon the Spirit is that such prayer exhibits a Trinitarian structure that makes clear the mediatorship of Christ. Moreover, the great blessing of the gospel is our adoption as the sons and daughters of God, and in that relation we can enter the communion of the Son with the Father using the very prayer language of the Son: namely, "Abba, Father" (see Mark 14:36; Rom. 8:15–16; Gal. 4:6–7). Praying to the Spirit is theologically permissible but would be unwise as the mainstay of one's praying. We are Christians, not "Pneumians." The Spirit in his role as the Paraclete has come to point us to Christ, not himself (John 15:26). To pray mainly to the Spirit may obscure the New Testament teaching on the mediatorship of Christ and his high priestly ministry as intercessor.[25]

Be Aspirational!

Having followed the present discussion up to this point, you may be wondering who is able to put things together this way. The fact is that there is an art to it. Art takes time to develop since

---

24. J. I. Packer, *Keep in Step with the Spirit* (Leicester, UK: Inter-Varsity Press, 1984), 261.

25. For a fuller discussion of this question, see Graham A. Cole, *Engaging with the Holy Spirit: Real Questions, Practical Answers* (Wheaton, IL: Crossway, 2008), chap. 3.

it involves knowledge, imagination, intuition, and skill. One of my sons is a university-trained visual artist. I have watched his art progress over the years since his graduation. I am impressed by the way he aspires to be better. The apostle called upon his younger associate Timothy to be aspirational (2 Tim. 2:15): "Do your best to present yourself to God as one approved, a worker who has no need to be ashamed, rightly handling the word of truth." The context is significant. The issue was false teaching. Hymenaeus and Philetus are named as false teachers who were claiming that the general resurrection was past. Timothy was not to be like them. Clearly, accuracy in doctrine, or teaching, was an apostolic aim. There is good reason for this. As Paul points out, the false teaching of Hymenaeus and Philetus was like gangrene and had in fact undermined the faith of some (2 Tim. 2:14–18). What a person believes matters. What a person teaches matters. Elsewhere, James's warning is sobering (James 3:1): "Not many of you should become teachers, my brothers, for you know that we who teach will be judged with greater strictness."

"Rightly handling the word of truth" ought to be the desire of any who hold a high view of the Bible's authority. In this context the primary reference is to the gospel. A road-making or farming metaphor may be informing Paul's counsel. The idea is of cutting a straight path or plowing in a straight line, as Chrysostom thought. To do so takes knowledge, skill, and dedicated time. The same is true of doing theology. As theologian Beth Felker Jones suggests, "Learning Christian doctrine is something like learning a new language: it takes time to learn the vocabulary and concepts used in Christian thought in order to understand what other people are saying."[26] If that is true

---

26. Beth Felker Jones, *Practicing Christian Doctrine: An Introduction to Thinking and Living Theologically* (Grand Rapids, MI: Baker Academic, 2014), 3. A great aid to learning the language of theology is Stanley J. Grenz, David Guretzki, and Cherith Fee Nordling, *Pocket Dictionary of Theological Terms* (Downers Grove, IL: InterVarsity Press, 1999).

of learning doctrine—and I believe it is—how much more is it true of doing theology in the way recommended in this work.

According to journalist Tom Weber:

> The great masters of the Renaissance—da Vinci, Michelangelo, et al.—if asked by the House of Medici, the Holy Father or any other influential patron of the visual arts to put a "rush job" on their masterpieces, would've probably dropped their palettes, chisels and other tools of the trade and wryly replied, "Rome wasn't built in a day."[27]

Neither is the theologian-pastor.[28]

The Way of Worship

Beth Felker Jones rightly maintains that "the study of doctrine is an act of love for God: in studying the things of God, we are formed as worshipers and as God's servants in the world."[29] But in biblical perspective, what is worship? The New Testament presents two main understandings of worship. We see in Revelation 4–5 our traditional understanding, which is the creaturely expression of the worth of God. These chapters offer a vision of the divine throne room, where both God and the Lamb of God (Jesus) are addressed in terms of worthiness. In Revelation 4:11 the cry is

> Worthy are you, our Lord and God,
> to receive glory and honor and power,

---

27. Tom Weber, "Rome Wasn't Built in a Day," ItalianNotebook (blog), April 22, 2013, http://www.italiannotebook.com/local-interest/origin-rome-wasnt-built-in-a-day/. Weber points out that the proverb predated da Vinci.

28. When I was a local church pastor, I was faced with the question of how to sustain the momentum which I had built up in theological college. I decided that I would read at least one solid Old Testament and New Testament commentary a year, a stretching work of doctrine (e.g., on the atonement), a volume of church history, a practical book of pastoral theology, and a spiritually challenging work addressed to my prayer life. I also decided to know all I could about the Sermon on the Mount (Matt. 5–7) and read it in Greek regularly.

29. Jones, *Practicing Christian Doctrine*, 3.

for you created all things,
>   and by your will they existed and were created.

In Revelation 5:9–10 we read,

Worthy are you to take the scroll
>   and to open its seals,
for you were slain, and by your blood you ransomed
>   people for God
>   from every tribe and language and people and nation,
and you have made them a kingdom and priests to
>   our God,
>   and they shall reign on the earth.

When God's people gather even to this day, it is an occasion to express corporately the worth of God.

There is another way that worship language is used in the New Testament. The apostle Paul calls upon the Roman Christians to respond to the mercies of God seen in the gospel, as set out in Romans 1–11, in the following way: "I appeal to you therefore, brothers, by the mercies of God, to present your bodies as a living sacrifice, holy and acceptable to God, which is your spiritual worship" (Rom. 12:1). Paul has the whole of the Christian life in mind as an offering to God. Later in the letter he speaks of his ministry to the Gentiles in worship language used in this extended way: "But on some points I have written to you very boldly by way of reminder, because of the grace given me by God to be a minister of Christ Jesus to the Gentiles in the priestly service of the gospel of God, so that the offering of the Gentiles may be acceptable, sanctified by the Holy Spirit" (Rom. 15:15–16).

This second understanding of what it is to worship is especially relevant to the task of doing theology. It is a task to be done in response to the gospel and offered to God as worship in this broad Pauline sense. To do so is to do theology as the way of worship, which is the fifth element in doing theology outside Eden. Importantly, the way of worship also addresses the danger of doing theology as a stimulating intellectual task only, a playing with abstract concepts, definitions, and distinctions.[30]

Conclusion

Putting things together is an important task in life. On the physical plane, think of IKEA's assemble-it-yourself furniture and the challenge of those instructions. (Why do I always seem to have screws left over?) Likewise, with regard to our theology or doctrine. Putting together all the relevant biblical testimonies and the relevant retrievals from church history while being mindful of our context requires great wisdom. It is a synthetic task—not in the sense of something artificial but in the sense of connecting things. The doctrine of God as Trinity provides an example for us. This task takes wisdom, and to be done properly, it also takes the requisite attitude toward God, which is reverence. Becoming better and better at the task takes time. And becoming better at doing theology ought to be our aspiration. Importantly, we offer this task to God as worship.

---

30. Yet again, we can learn from the witness of Christian thought and practice. Anselm of Canterbury did not fall into the danger of mere intellectualism, as can be seen in his classic work *Proslogion*, which is in the form of a prayer as his faith sought understanding. See Anselm, *Proslogion*, http://www.stanselminstitute.org/files/AnselmProslogion .pdf, accessed December 13, 2017.

Conclusion

As a theological teacher, I tell my students, "Whether you are writing an essay or a thesis, the trick is to say what you are going to say in the introduction, then say it, and at the end say that you have said it." So, what have I tried to say in this short work on theological method?

God has spoken. The Bible is where the divine self-revelation is to be found. Theology is both reflection upon that self-revelation as the word of God and a response to it. Doing theology is a human activity that is always open to being reformed by the word of God. This is because Scripture, as the word of revelation, is the norm of norms. In any contest between authorities, Scripture is the final court of appeal. It is the touchstone of faith. Tradition, reason, and experience have their roles, but they are ruled norms that are ruled by Scripture. They are never to displace Scripture as the norm of norms. However, Scripture needs interpretation. On this score, the legacy of the Reformers of the sixteenth century remains immensely valuable. The analogy of faith provides excellent guidelines still for the interpreter, especially when nuanced with genre analysis.

Theology is not done in a vacuum, however. We do our theology in fellowship with those of the past (e.g., Calvin) and the present (e.g., Kevin J. Vanhoozer). In other words, we do not read Scripture and do theology informed by Scripture as though no other Christians have ever lived, as though there were no witness of Christian thought and practice. Doing theology is a situated pursuit. We live outside Eden in the world of human brokenness. This is the truth in the postmodern perspective, but human imagination happily can give us a critical distance from ourselves, even despite our finiteness and fallenness. How these elements are to be connected in a mutually informing way that preserves the supremacy of Scripture as the word of God is the work of wisdom as opposed to foolishness. Putting the elements together is a work of faithful reason. The faithful theologian fears the Lord and endeavors to be an excellent phenomenologist when it comes to reading the text.

Having said all the above, I must emphasize that rigidity in method needs to be avoided. What do I mean by that? In this work I have followed what I contend to be the logical order in doing theology (*ordo essendi*, "essential order"). However, given life's circumstances, the order may change in the actual doing (*ordo cognoscendi*, "knowing order"). For example, some new theory as to who we are that arises from the world of human brokenness should send us back to the Scriptures (word of revelation) for our theological anthropology. A case in point is the sexuality question. Is our sexuality fluid? Can someone be a male trapped in a female body? How is gender dysphoria to be faced? Have these questions been addressed before in the history of theological discussion (witness of Christian thought and practice)? If so, when and how successfully were they addressed?

Bringing these elements into conversation with each other is the work of wisdom, one would hope, from beginning to end. Notice that with regard to the sexuality issue before us, this process of theological reflection would begin not with Scripture but with our setting and its urgent questions, then move to the witness of Christian thought and practice, and to the historic Christian understanding of our anthropology, before revisiting the questions of human identity and sexuality in the light of God's self-revelation.

This brief work has offered a way to do theology, a method, involving all the elements mentioned above. However, if the discussion stopped here, a vital dimension would be missed. The divine project outside of Eden and this side of the fall is nothing less than the restoration of true worship throughout creation. Worship has a corporate dimension, as we have seen, in Revelation 4–5. God's creatures are gathered and express the worth of God. This is the traditional understanding of worship (i.e., expressing the "worth-ship" of God). However, we have also seen that there is a more radical understanding to be found in the New Testament witness. Recall how the great apostle Paul reworks Old Testament worship categories such that the whole of the Christian life when lived out in response to the gospel is worship, as Romans 12:1–2 makes plain. To use Luther's luminous phrase, life is lived *coram Deo* (before God). Our doing theology needs to be offered daily to God, which is our reasonable worship. That way, for the theologian, Sunday in church connects with Monday in the study.

Doing theology then is a way of loving God with our minds, hopefully renewed minds in the Pauline sense. We do theology as disciples of Christ.[1] Justo L. González makes this valuable comment concerning theological education:

> No seminary professor or ecclesiastical leader knows what will be the new circumstances that the church and its

---

1. Kevin J. Vanhoozer, "From Bible to Theology," in *Theology, Church, and Ministry*, ed. David S. Dockery (Nashville: B&H Academic, 2017), 233, makes this valuable point about the goal of theological education, which applies here as well: "[It is] to understand God and God's Word truly in order to live out our citizenship of the gospel under the lordship of Jesus Christ."

members will face in the near future. If we are to prepare leaders for a future that we cannot fully envision, it does not suffice to teach them how to think and what to do. They also have to be trained in such a way that they will know how to respond to unexpected circumstances and challenges on the basis of solid theological and biblical principles. If we don't prepare such leaders, when those circumstances and challenges arrive the church will not know how to respond to them, and in consequence it will seem irrelevant and will be increasingly marginalized.[2]

May this discussion help prevent the irrelevancy which González fears. It will do so if we make it our aim to know the Scriptures, to have a working understanding of the Christian past, to be aware of the groaning creation in which we live, to think wisely, and to offer all such practices to God in worshipful response to the God of grace met in the gospel of Jesus Christ.

---

2. Justo L. González, *The History of Theological Education* (Nashville: Abingdon, 2015), 121.

Further Reading

Clark, David K. *To Know and Love God: Method of Theology.* Wheaton, IL: Crossway, 2010. A deep book for the more advanced reader.

Grenz, Stanley J., and Roger E. Olson. *Who Needs Theology? An Invitation to the Study of God.* Downers Grove, IL: InterVarsity Press; 1996. A simple and very practical introduction to theology. Chapter 5 is especially helpful.

Kapic, Kelly M. *A Little Book for New Theologians: Why and How to Study Theology.* Downers Grove, IL: IVP Academic, 2012. Particularly strong on the virtues needed by the budding theologian.

Sproul, R. C. *Knowing Scripture.* 3rd ed. Downers Grove, IL: InterVarsity Press, 2016. Simply written but full of good sense and helpful insights.

Thielicke, Helmut. *A Little Exercise for Young Theologians.* Translated by Charles L. Taylor. Grand Rapids, MI: Eerdmans, 1978. A classic—brief but pointed.

Vanhoozer, Kevin J. "From Bible to Theology." In *Theology, Church, and Ministry*, ed. David S. Dockery, 233–56. Nashville: B&H Academic, 2017. Written with his usual flair for language and freshness of expression.

General Index

Scripture Index